PRAISE FOR
NO NAME BASTARD

"Imagine taking the significant moments from your life, distilling them down to the crucial lessons you've learned, and sharing these practical and actionable insights so others may benefit. That is what Tori has achieved. I double-dare you to read this amazing book."

—**ROBERT A. GOLDBERG**, founding partner,
Organization Insight

"In this insightful and beautifully written book, Tori guides us through her pivotal life lessons, granting us the opportunity to reflect and examine our own challenges and the insights they offer. She emphasizes that we alone determine our responses to events: with self-awareness, emotional accountability, and deliberate choices that shape our future and influence those around us. By separating what we can control from what we can influence, we unlock the freedom to lead ourselves toward a more self-directed life. Tori's narrative powerfully illustrates that each experience—whether uplifting or challenging—can foster growth if we are willing to learn from the life lessons it offers."

—**KARL KUHNERT, PhD**, professor of the practice,
Goizueta Business School at Emory University

"Tori DaCosta does a masterful job of sharing her honest and vulnerable life journey while provoking readers to reflect on their own life experiences and look for those nuggets of hope. This book is a masterclass in balancing struggle with inspiration, and realness with practical life lessons. I highly recommend this book to anyone looking for light in the midst of darkness or hope in a season of hopelessness. Inspiring to the very end!"

—**BRANDON SMITH**, host, *The Workplace Therapist Show*; president, The Worksmiths LLC.

"This book gives language and courage to two muscles we all need: saying no and hearing no. With a little humor, a lot of humility, and hard-won wisdom, DaCosta shows us how to release what isn't ours and own what is. A brave, practical guide for anyone ready to lead with clarity, compassion, and conviction."

—**LATRAYL ADAMS, MS**, director of counseling and well-being, Winston-Salem/Forsyth County Schools

NO NAME BASTARD

NO NAME BASTARD

HOW OUR LIVES TEACH US
WHAT WE CAN CONTROL,
MANAGE, AND INFLUENCE

TORI DACOSTA

GREENLEAF
BOOK GROUP PRESS

This book is intended as a reference volume only. It is sold with the understanding that the publisher and author are not engaged in rendering any professional services. The information given here is designed to help you make informed decisions. If you suspect that you have a problem that might require professional treatment or advice, you should seek competent help.

Published by Greenleaf Book Group Press
Austin, Texas
www.gbgpress.com

Distributed by Greenleaf Book Group

For ordering information or special discounts for bulk purchases, please contact Greenleaf Book Group at PO Box 91869, Austin, TX 78709, 512.891.6100.

Design and composition by Greenleaf Book Group
Cover design by Greenleaf Book Group
Cover images used under licence from © Adobestock.com

Publisher's Cataloging-in-Publication data is available.

Print ISBN: 979-8-88645-457-4

eBook ISBN: 979-8-88645-458-1

To offset the number of trees consumed in the printing of our books, Greenleaf donates a portion of the proceeds from each printing to the Arbor Day Foundation. Greenleaf Book Group has replaced over 50,000 trees since 2007.

Printed in the United States of America on acid-free paper

26 27 28 29 30 31 32 33 10 9 8 7 6 5 4 3 2 1

First Edition

This book is dedicated to those who are inspired by life's challenges, the ones who get up after being knocked down and have the courage to lead as their authentic selves.

CONTENTS

INTRODUCTION

MOST DAYS IN LIFE ARE just not that memorable. We wake up, go through our morning routine, tackle the day, wind down, and do it all over again. The days simply fade into phases of time unless something disrupts the rhythm of the mundane and encapsulates it as a memory. Think of your morning ritual or that thing you do every Friday night. It's just a part of life. The daily commute is procedural until the day there is a fender bender. The weekend family movie nights, complete with everyone's favorite snacks, are another stitch in the fabric of quality time—until someone chokes and needs the Heimlich maneuver. Those divergent days create "remember when" stories because they are more pronounced than all the other days when you did the exact same thing. The other, less eventful days were the norm.

The fender bender story is mine. The choking one is too. All the monotonous days are a part of shaping who we are and how we navigate this world, but the "remember when" days, they are a part of our story. These are the tales we relive at family gatherings and recount to our children. They are the moments that create lifelong bonds with the people we experienced them with. If we pay attention, these memories teach us lessons about how we traverse our environment, and with a little self-awareness, they can help us understand who we are.

So many of the qualities that define us must be earned. Confidence, resilience, and wisdom usually come with a few scrapes and bruises. For me, there were times when the scrapes and bruises were literal, but oftentimes the path to those earned qualities is a matter of getting back up after we've been knocked down and moving forward when we want to quit. This book will help you do just that.

You may have chosen this book because you're curious. Perhaps you are reading it because someone recommended it. Either way, you may be wondering why you should go on this journey with me. First, I am a person just like you. I've had more than enough and barely enough. I've experienced health and sickness. I've had my heart broken, and I've experienced some of the greatest joys that love offers. I know what it feels like to succeed, and I know what it feels like to fail. I've helped individuals transform their lives, and I've led teams to success. Perhaps more important because of its foundational relevance personally and in the marketplace, I understand the need to lead oneself well. Success looks different to different people, and individuals have their own definition of success, but I have never seen a version that did not require personal growth.

INTRODUCTION

I am going to share several "remember when" stories with you. These moments have been seared so firmly in my memory that I can recall every detail. Some were so painful that I (literally) could not see. My hope is that as you read my stories and the lessons I learned from each experience, you will be reminded of a few lessons of your own and perhaps learn some new ones. My experiences point to areas where I underwent personal growth—areas such as identity, connection, and tenacity. Lessons often come in layers, and some of my stories have overlapping undercurrents, just as I'm sure your stories do.

My greatest hope is that you will discover that you are stronger and more resilient than you ever thought you could be and that you will allow challenges to be the fuel that ignites the best version of you.

Stories have a way of helping us connect with the pain and joy felt by others and, sometimes, the pain and joy within ourselves. Life is a great teacher if we are willing to learn. Too many people have amazing stories that never get told, and this means we're missing out on opportunities to connect on a deeper, more meaningful level. Our stories reveal our experiences, beliefs, and gifts. They can also reveal what makes us unique. Your stories empower you when you share them, and they have the power to inspire others. Inspiration changes lives and can serve as the catalyst driving positive change when we are presented with life's bifurcation points.

You've probably heard that there are two things guaranteed in life—death and taxes. (Benjamin Franklin gets credit for that one.) I'll add a third—challenges. They come in different shapes, sizes, and degrees of difficulty, and they are a part of the human experience. Between my time living in New York and then North Carolina with a short stint in the Midwest, I attended six schools by the sixth grade. I had to learn to adapt to new people and environments quickly. There was a time when I would have said I've had my fair share of challenges. Perhaps you feel you've had yours.

But then I wondered, what *is* my fair share of challenges? What is your fair share? How many is too many? For that matter, how do you define a challenge? Is a challenge simply an opportunity? Our challenges (or opportunities) may be different, but they have the potential to produce something within us that might not have been fostered otherwise; I'm referring to good, life-enhancing qualities like gratitude, discipline, resilience, and even greatness.

I appreciate a good challenge, but I have not always appreciated the prospect to become the best version of myself. I've shied away from uncomfortable conversations and anything that made me feel vulnerable.

This is a recipe for playing it safe, and playing it safe usually means playing small. You may wonder, what's the problem with playing it safe? What difference does it make if we choose to play small? That margin is our potential, and when realized, it means living a fulfilling and impactful life.

We get to make decisions that allow us to become the best version of ourselves, and when we do, we quickly learn that many factors are beyond our control. Over time, I realized that to have peace and clarity in the process, I needed to learn what I could manage, what I could control, and what I could influence.

An equally important learning was how I could grow on this journey called life. I had to be willing to embrace discomfort and therefore *embrace* challenges. I encourage you to embrace them as well. It's my hope that this book will provide an opportunity for you to inch (or leap!) closer to the best version of yourself through learning about my experiences and reflecting on your own.

Names have been omitted to protect the guilty (and the innocent). There is usually more than one perspective in a shared experience, and I acknowledge that in writing this book, I have the advantage of sharing solely my own. The lessons learned are mine as well, and I hope that they encourage, inspire, or ground you. Maybe even all three!

Perhaps you will have a lightbulb moment and make connections between the lessons I've learned and moments in your own life. To facilitate this, I have included a pondering page at the end of each chapter where you can record your thoughts and opportunities for growth. Be sure to take advantage of this!

Framing your own experiences based on what you can control, manage, and influence may bring you an additional layer of clarity with growth. We have the ability to control outcomes tethered to our decisions, manage our mental and emotional responses, and influence outcomes when others are involved.

I'll share insights on how this applied to my experiences, which may help you as you learn from you own.

I once had a professor who said that childhood experiences influence how we show up in life. He went on to say that during his formative years, his home had been full of conflict and he assumed the role of peacemaker, attempting to keep everyone happy so the fighting would stop. As a result, he became a conflict-averse adult.

I too am confident that the person I am today was partly molded by the experiences shared in this book. They have shaped the kind of mom, sister, daughter, friend, cousin, teammate, leader, neighbor, businesswoman, and spouse I've grown to become, and it's fair to acknowledge that I am still growing.

I hope these pages inspire you to grow right along with me.

CHAPTER 1

NO

No: Not at all; to no extent.[1]

I SPENT WAY TOO MANY years in the naive lane. Naivety is a close cousin to gullibility, and Mr. Naive, Ms. Gullible, and I were all good friends. I took people at their word and experienced disappointment many times. Not only did I assume someone's intention was honest, but I also assumed it was positive. I would have done well in the "no contract needed, your handshake will do" generation.

Several years ago, I was forced to face my gullible self and do some reflecting. I learned about a man given a task that did not

---

1 All definitions, including this one, sourced from Google's English dictionary provided by Oxford Languages unless otherwise indicated.

turn out well because of his failure to say one simple word—no. I'll share more about him in a moment, but I want to tell you about the time I should have said no but didn't.

A water gun called the Super Soaker was the hot new toy to hit the market in the early 1990s. Kids everywhere ran around soaking each other in the summer sun. There were several kids in my neighborhood, and our water gun battles got so intense that when the dust settled, we often looked as if we had just climbed out of a swimming pool.

Somehow lines were drawn, and the emerging factions were boys versus girls. Both sides had to be ready at all times. There were organized battles, ambushes, skirmishes, and retreats for cover that usually meant someone ran home with hopes of you chasing them so they could grab their water hose and douse you into submission. It was pure fun.

The day I ended up on crutches started out like any other summer day in the South—hot! One of the girls in the neighborhood was learning to drive and thought a car could be a game changer in the water gun wars. A couple of middle school amigas came to my home and said we were going to ambush the boys with a drive-by. (Keep in mind, it's only water.) Now, there is an expectation that a licensed driver must be in the car when someone is learning to drive, usually a parent, and I knew my mom would not approve of me getting in the car unless there was an experienced driver along for the ride. I was assured that the new driver's mom would be in the car and gained my mom's approval for the joyride. (I failed to mention the planned ambush. Omission can be just as bad as commission.)

Our neighborhood was not large. There was one main artery with several shorter perpendicular streets (shaped like a comb), so getting to any street was easy. We made the short trek to the rally point and readied an array of water weapons, one of them being a long, narrow plunger that had to be filled with a bucket. This became my weapon for the day, and the only way to shoot it was to point it in the direction of the victim and push hard on the rear handle, forcing all the water out of the front. One shot was all I had, so I knew I'd better make it count. As we all stood waiting to get in the vehicle, our new practicing driver walked toward the car, solo. I paused and asked about her mom accompanying us. She said her mom gave her permission to go without her. I felt a hesitation.

Allow me a side note to expound on that hesitancy. I paused as I stood at that car door because I had told my mom there would be another mom in the car. My conscience began bothering me and I wrestled with it:

> *Tori, you should not get in that car. You told your mom that her mom would be in the car, and clearly, she is not.*
>
> True . . . but you're just going a few blocks over. You're not even leaving the neighborhood.
>
> *If you get in that car, you lied. That is not what you told your mom.*

Yeah . . . but you just filled up this behemoth of a water gun soaker. You are ready for battle.

My thoughts were interrupted by the sound of car doors opening. I don't know if her mom joining us was ever a part of the plan, and it didn't matter. The choice was mine to own. I opened the door and got in. I told myself, *You're only going two blocks over. It'll be a quick sneak attack, and you'll be back to the rally point in no time.*

I sat on the rear passenger side with the long plunger resting across the span of the back seat, covering me and my battle companion's legs. It was almost too big for one person and a bit cumbersome for middle-school-sized me to manage. We were excited about the ambush that we were moments from pulling off. My battle buddies and I got quiet as we drove down the road designed like the spine of the comb. I sat still as the sedan rounded the corner onto the street with the house where we knew we would find the boys. As the car approached, I was shocked to see that every boy in the neighborhood was sitting on the porch. All of them! We had battled each of them from time to time but not all at once. It appeared that they were just hanging out, and they were not immediately alarmed when they saw us. The reality was we were all friends and none of us had ever driven up in a car. This could have easily been a benevolent visit, but the moment the first weapon breached the car window in their direction, it was like kicking a hive. They leaped off the porch and ran in our direction.

CHAPTER 1: NO

My weapon was too big to maneuver through the window, so I opened the door. Just as I stepped out of the car, the driver panicked and called for a retreat. It felt like a squad of soldiers were racing toward us. I quickly ducked back into the car, but there was one problem: I wasn't fully inside as the car began to move. My left leg and most of my body were safely within the vehicle, but the sedan door was still open as I attempted to bring the water gun and my right leg to safety as well. In the blink of an eye, the back tire trapped my right foot as the car moved forward. I yelled, "Stop!"

The wheel kept moving slowly, and the back of my foot slipped out of the shoe as the sole of my sneaker gave way to the weight of the grinding tire. I fought to keep the front of my foot in the sneaker. My right leg submitted to the demand of the pressure, forcing me into a split stance as my leg angled back and my knee tilted closer to the ground. The exposed inner heel of my now flexed foot pressed against the road. The only barrier between my foot and the pavement was a sock.

"Stop! Stop!"

But as the wheel kept moving, I felt the rough pavement quickly rub away the sock and begin to abrade my skin. My heel bone pressed to the ground as the sneaker that barely hung on served as the only barrier of protection between my foot and the tire.

By now the other passengers realized what was happening and we all yelled, "Stop! Stop! Stop!" My gaze lifted briefly as I pulled my leg into the car. The sneaker stayed with the tire, and all the guys were frozen with looks of shock on their faces. We had only moved a few feet. I looked down at my foot and saw a hole the size of a quarter. It was deep. The skin and everything familiar were gone. Layers of tissue that were never meant to be seen were jagged and exposed. It began filling up with blood and spilling over. I remember thinking, *This is bad.*

The driver headed in the direction of my street, and although it was only one block over, we could not get there quickly enough. She parked in front of my house, and two of my friends helped me out of the car. They placed my arms around their shoulders as I hopped up the driveway to the door. Tears were streaming down my face as blood left evidence of every step we took.

I remember my mother's face when she opened the door. I never wanted to see that look on her face again, not caused by me or anyone else. My friends and my mom helped me hop into the kitchen and carefully settle in a chair. My mother called an ambulance, and it seemed like forever before they arrived, but they wasted no time once they were in the door. They assessed my foot and cut my jeans straight up the leg. Within minutes we were off to the emergency room.

My mother sat by my side while I lay on the bed in the ER. I explained to her what happened, and to the attendant, and the nurse, and then again to the doctor. Over and over, I had to explain why I had a hole in my foot. My mother was upset, but she could see that I was suffering for my mistake, so no need to make me feel worse. In one day, I told a half-truth to my mom, lost one of my favorite sneakers, managed to get a hole in my foot, and was now lying in the emergency room with a head full of sweat-frizzed hair and a pair of blood-stained, one-legged jeans neatly folded beside me. It was quite a day for a barely teen girl. There was no victory to celebrate, and no reliving the highlight reel of soaking superiority. There was only an unforeseen injury, a stressed mother, and a trip to the emergency room.

I was just beginning to come to terms with the consequences of my misjudgment and failure to say no when the nurse walked into the room, sat a kit on a small table, and walked out. I could see big black letters in all caps across the top—GRAFT. My heart started racing. I looked at my mom and started asking questions. When the nurse returned, I asked him more questions. He informed me that the doctor would decide if I needed a skin graft, and when I asked where the skin would come from, he began to describe how they would likely take skin from my buttocks and graft it to my foot. I already knew that I would not be able to walk, and now I was worried about not being able to sit.

In the end, the skin graft never happened. I do not know if the graft was really a consideration, but if it wasn't, the doctor did a good job making sure I learned my lesson, along with spending the rest of the summer on crutches. I even started the school year on crutches. My mom had to help me with day-to-day activities, and simple tasks like bathing became difficult because at all costs I had to keep the dressing on my foot dry, which is a bit ironic, since it was my poor decision regarding water that earned the dry foot requirement.

Some of the guys were kind enough to check on me, and one delivered the sneaker left behind during the incident—a far cry from Cinderella's glass slipper story. The rubber sole looked as if it had lost a battle against a grinder. It was no match for the tire and the pavement, and I couldn't help but think how severe the injury would have been if I had been wearing a sandal or flip-flop. Suddenly, I was very thankful for that destroyed shoe. I kept it for a short time after the incident so I wouldn't forget, then I realized the scar on my foot (that remains today) would suffice.

Several years after the foot incident, I learned about the man I mentioned earlier—the one given the task that did not turn out well because he failed to say no. His assignment was straightforward, but a colleague convinced him that his orders were changed and diverted his plans. Instead of saying no and sticking to the original plan (or even checking to confirm the change), he followed his all-too-trusting nature before learning that he was deceived. Unfortunately, his safety was compromised in his attempt to complete his mission, and he lost his life.

Thankfully, this is not your story or mine, but I was appalled when I heard it. The man who was too trusting believed a lie and paid with his life.

Could life really be that unfair . . . that cruel? Yes. His story would have been different if he had simply said no.

Learning about this man's experience hit me hard because I would have responded the same way he did. I would have trusted the lying colleague and paid with my life. I would have thought, *We're on the same team; of course he has my back.* Wrong! Spending a summer on crutches pales in comparison to his consequence, but this made me realize I *must* get better at saying no.

Saying No—It's a Process

I wish I could tell you that I became a pro at saying no after the foot fiasco, but it took some time. There were still more lessons to learn. No is hard for many people to say. (It's also hard for many people to hear.) The word "no" and I have a special relationship. I am 100 percent certain that I have not said it enough, and I have persistently pushed past it more times than I can count.

Aside from being too trusting, I was also a people pleaser. It was several years before I learned this about myself, and when I realized it, I quickly learned that people-pleasing plus not being good at saying no was an awful combination. I felt obligated to deliver on my word and was dedicated once I said yes, even if the yes was reluctant.

People are inclined to take the path of least resistance, and I don't think most of the requests made of me were because folks realized I struggled with saying no; they just knew I would be an easy yes. This is a recipe to be asked first and often. I said yes to things that I did not want to say yes to because I was not sure how to say no. As an adult, some of those yeses opened doors to great opportunities—and others led to headaches.

Having a hard time saying no might sound ridiculous to someone who has never struggled with this. Has this been an area of struggle for you? I salute you if saying no has never been a challenge for you or you have never been plagued with people-pleasing. I felt like I needed a reason to say no or I had to have a prior obligation that kept me from being available for the new request. It was easy to say no to people I perceived as rude, disrespectful, or unkind. The yes was nearly automatic if I was fond of or respected the person making the request.

Unfortunately, the need (or want) for downtime, being tired, or simply not having a desire to do whatever was asked of me were not valid reasons to say no. I remember the feeling of relief if someone asked me to do something I did not want to do and I could confidently say no because I had already committed to something else. We have only so many hours in a day and limited time on this earth. Imagine taking care of everyone else's to-dos while your dreams get pushed so far to the side that they die!

One day I heard someone proclaim that *no* is a complete sentence, no explanation needed. That was the day my mindset began to shift. I did not have to justify the no with reasons, and no prior obligation needed to hold space on my calendar. My lack of interest or desire to carry out the task was enough.

Accepting No—It's a Process

Saying no takes one set of muscles, and hearing no takes another. I could not stand for my mother to tell me no when I was a kid, especially when I wanted to play outside. I figured out how to get her to say yes when she preferred for me to stay close to the nest. I waited until she was very tired and preparing to take a nap. I'd quietly walk into the room and ask if I could go outside to play with my friends. If she was on the front end of winding down for her nap and more alert, she would respond "no," and I'd plead with her until she said yes just to get rid of me. If she was on the back end of settling down, the answer was usually a soft yes. I'd run outside immediately, because although I knew it was not a fully committed yes, it was a yes. When I returned home sweaty and hungry after several rounds of freeze tag, Simon Says, or kickball, she would peer at me and ask, "Who told you that you could go outside?" I'd smile and confidently say, "You did." It didn't take her long to catch on to my nap plan, and then there was no way to circumvent the no.

I learned as an adult that the world is full of rejection, and no one is as loving as your mother. I had to adjust quickly when I started working in sales and the nos flowed like honey in a beehive. When I was a kid, the word "no" felt like a personal rejection. That was cured in one day by a rude, angry customer. I could not tell you what he was angry about because his request was not fully coherent through all the profanity. I had never heard anyone put so many curse words into sentences that still made sense. (I still haven't to this day.) I just happened to be the person who answered the phone, and that man gave me a tongue-lashing like nothing I had ever experienced.

Turns out, it was one of the best things that could have happened to me. I did not know him, I'd had zero interaction with him prior to that moment, and here he was, insanely angry—at me. Although I had nothing to do with whatever he was upset about, I was the recipient of his fury. I politely told him I could not help him until he calmed down. I also told him I was going to hang up and advised him to call back when he cooled off. That man cursed and yelled that I'd better not hang up on him. I did—and no surprise, he called back immediately.

He taught me a valuable lesson that day—it wasn't about me. He taught me not to take rejection or rude behavior personally. Someone may be having a bad day (or a bad life), they may have received upsetting news, they could be ill, their kids could be getting on their nerves, they might be in physical pain, they could have just lost their job, and so on. They could also just be an ugly human being. But that day I learned that whatever was going on with him had *nothing* to do with me.

It was a lightbulb moment. He wasn't the first person I encountered who treated me poorly; he was just the first who was so egregious when we'd had no prior interaction. Suddenly, I realized that it wasn't personal, and it wasn't my burden to carry.

What a freeing realization! This made it so much easier for me to hear no, both personally and professionally—whether it's a simple straight-up no or an unwarranted rude rant.

Not every no response is attached to rude behavior, and I became better at hearing the casual "I don't want to," "I don't feel like it," or "I'm not interested" types of nos as well.

I learned that I can only control me, so I made sure I did my part by being kind and respectful. In the professional realm, I made sure people were well informed and knew their options. People have a right to say no, and I had to be okay with that.

They own their yes or no, I own mine, and you own yours. We all have a right to our decision, and the reality is we also get to own the consequences of those choices—positive or negative.

I had to own my failure to say no the day of the water gun battle. I also had to live with the consequences and the inconvenience caused to the people who helped me through my injury. It was an important and jarring lesson to learn, and weeks of dealing with an inoperable foot is plenty of time to reflect.

Learning What I Could Control

Yes, You Can Say No

There are several ways to say no, and some are easier than others, but you can do it, and I can help you. If you struggle in this area, you may find these ideas helpful. They may even inspire you to develop your own no responses.

- Simply say "no" or "no thank you"—full stop. These are complete responses, capable of standing alone. They do not need an excuse or a reason to accompany them. This requires confidence, and if you are not at this level yet, it's a place to work toward.

- Pass it back or enlist support. It can be hard to say no when someone volunteers you for a task in a group setting. You may feel called out or put on the spot. For instance, you are in a meeting, and everyone decides a new project needs to be implemented. Your classmate or colleague says that you would be great and volunteers you to lead it. Simply apply a rule I practice: If you "voluntell" someone else, you are really volunteering yourself. You can politely say, "Now (insert name), you know when you volunteer someone else, you're really volunteering yourself." They'll likely smile at your creative no.

- Let's say you don't mind taking on the task. If you want to complete the project but would appreciate some help, you can also say, "Sure, I'll do it if you are on board to help me." (This works in the personal arena as well.) There will be professional situations where you will be "voluntold," and even though you usually cannot give a blanket no in those situations without consequence, it does not hurt to inquire about resources available to support you and recruit other dedicated individuals to help expedite the work. Yes at work can foster positive life changes, so use your nos sparingly and with discretion.
- "Not right now," "not at this time," or "let me think about it and get back to you" are great temporary no phrases if they are honest. The request may be something you genuinely want to fulfill, but you are not in the right season of life to make it happen. No does not have to be permanent. "Tell me more about what's required" is also a good way to flesh out details to help you make your decision. You can even

ask if that person has requested help from anyone else at that point.

I do not recommend using the "let me think about it" option unless you really want to think about it. Don't waste your or the other person's time by biding time. I've lived in a few states along the Eastern Seaboard. Compared to the North, the South is known to be slower. (It is generally easier to find parking, too.) Culturally, the nos can even be slow. These phrases can be used as a no-in-waiting because oftentimes the deliverer deems it too impolite to offer a direct no. Bless our hearts. A quick no is better than wasted time, and if you don't want to be a part of whatever is being requested, simply make that clear.

Avoid the No-Risk No

This chapter is all about empowering the no, but there are instances when no is not the best response. Too often the no is motivated by the fear of making a mistake or anticipating a less-than-ideal outcome. There is no danger of harm, just the potential for a bruised ego. If this is the only reason for your no, think again. You may be missing an opportunity. There will be times when you just have to go for it, because sometimes we must take a chance to grow.

You may have to push through some anxiety to take that chance, but the lesson is worth it. Here are a few questions to ask yourself that may help you along the way.

- Am I passionate about what is being asked of me?
- Does this present an opportunity to learn and grow?
- What would I be doing if not this?
- Do I have the capacity (mental and emotional)?
- Do I have the expertise needed, and is it detrimental if I don't?
- Is there room for me to learn without damaging outcomes?
- Can others help or support me?

Too often we respond without considering the consequences or how an action impacts other areas of our life. Maturity and wisdom give us the opportunity to be more intentional in our evaluation. As a kid, my year was measured by nine-week grading periods and summer breaks. As an adult, it's marked by quarterly increments and holidays. I take time every twelve weeks to assess what is going well and identify areas that need improvement. Occasionally, this includes making a list of activities that I will either continue to devote time, energy, and resources to or for which I will create an exit strategy. The exit strategy may include notifying stakeholders of my intended timeline and identifying and preparing a replacement. Assessing your nos and yeses is a good way to declutter your life. Too many little yeses (that should be nos) steal from vital "go for it" yeses.

Focus on What You Can Control

One of my high school teachers had a large printed quote on the wall that was perfectly placed for all to see. I read it daily. She was the no-nonsense, no-excuse type. In most classes I could tell which students the teacher favored. This teacher favored no one. She demanded our best effort and ownership of our results. The quote read:

> "Watch your thoughts; they become words. Watch your words; they become actions. Watch your actions; they become habits. Watch your habits; they become character. Watch your character; it becomes your destiny."
>
> —LAO-TZU

Reading that quote every day taught me that I have 100 percent ownership of my choices, and those choices control outcomes. I may not be able to control everything that happens to me, but I can choose how I respond. As a child, I thought becoming an adult granted automatic maturity and wisdom. If you've been on earth for a while, you know this is not true. We all get older. We don't all get wiser. Some people do not take ownership for their lives, their choices, or even how they treat other people.

The Golden Rule says to do unto others as you would have them do unto you. It is a baseline for respect and kindness. I came to the realization that this rule assumes we all have the same value system, which may not be true in today's world. It also assumes positive intent and that the executor of the Golden Rule is concerned about personal interactions. I have learned that if someone does not care about the outcome of their day (or their life), the likelihood of them caring about yours or mine is low. The intent of the Golden Rule is mutual respect and love for the people we encounter. I believe most people are inherently good and care about others; however, there are people in this world who, for an array of reasons, are not kind or respectful. We may be able to influence them, but we cannot control them.

It is not easy to be kind when someone is rude. It is equally challenging to be respectful when you feel you've been disrespected. I encourage us (yes, us . . . you and me) not to let the behavior of others change how we treat people.

Don't let it impact taking ownership for your choices. Have you ever heard someone say, "I got so mad at (insert name) that they made me (insert the behavior that was a result of the anger, i.e., hit, smack, curse, etc.)"? I am not implying that choosing our response is by any means easy, but we are not puppets. We get to choose. You have the power to be a ray of positivity when someone else's light is not shining bright. I am not suggesting you become a doormat, but focus on what you can control—and the one thing you can control is you.

Learning What I Could Influence

Plan Before You Play

Although I never should have gotten in the car for the drive-by battle that day, I learned far more than the importance of saying no. I also learned the importance of thinking ahead about possible outcomes.

My battle buddies and I simply grabbed our weapons and jumped in the car. We did not orchestrate the plan of attack, the angle of our weapons, or how we would respond to a counterattack. Our plan was to drive up and shoot our water guns in the direction of the boys. Clearly, that did not work out well. The need for strategy was less obvious on the day of the water gun war debacle because I did not have the foresight to plan ahead or the wisdom to weigh the consequences if things went badly.

More often than not, personally and professionally, we have time to formulate our game plan. This allows us to identify the desired result(s), tap into the strength of team members, determine how to execute, and plan for the unexpected. The plan may not be perfect, but at least you will have one and can adjust if needed. Not too many people do well flying by the seat of their pants or winging it. Greatness does not happen by accident, but injuries do.

Silence Is Golden

For many years I was uncomfortable with prolonged silence, which sometimes led me to respond yes when I really preferred to stay quiet and say no.

I had the pleasure of sitting in a session with Dr. Julie Bell, the founder and president of the organization The Mind of a Champion. She is masterful at waiting seven seconds to give people time to respond. If you have ever asked a question and then sat quietly for seven seconds as you waited for an answer, you'll probably agree that it feels like much longer than seven seconds. Trust me; that feeling will pass. With practice, you too can be a master of the seven seconds of silence. It will become so easy that you'll be able to handle much longer.

In fact, I recommend trying it right now. Lift your gaze above the pages and look straight at whatever is in front of you as if you are staring into another person's eyes. Count 1 Mississippi, 2 Mississippi, 3 Mississippi . . . all the way to 7 Mississippi silently. Next time try it with a real person or group after you ask a question. Don't give in to the temptation to fill the void by speaking.

I have gotten plenty of practice silently counting to seven in one-on-one and group meetings. I have practiced it enough to know that silence makes people uncomfortable. I can empathize because I was that person. Many people feel the need to break the silence. There is a saying that silence is deafening, and if you have ever played the quiet game with a child, you know how hard it is to keep our mouths shut.

I decided to teach a group of twenty-plus adults to do this in a meeting. I stood in front of the room wearing a shirt that read "but did you die" and let them know that silence is okay and to prove that no one would die, we were going to practice it. Some of their faces displayed stress at the thought of sitting silently, and they did not even have to leave their seats. The discomfort was palpable for a few participants as we looked at each other without speaking. The good news is everyone made it to seven seconds, and no one died.

A moment of pause allows you and others to listen and think, and there are countless ways to get real-life practice. One way is to ask a thoughtful question during a conversation and pause. Slow down and make space for the other person. There is a difference between stopping to listen and waiting to speak. You can also couple practicing silence and saying no. The next time you are in a room of fully capable people, and no one wants to take on responsibility for a new task (including you), it is okay to be quiet and not feel the need to respond. If no one wants to handle the task, perhaps it is time to evaluate its importance. It may be worthwhile to outsource or redirect energy and resources. The challenge could also be that the right people are not in the room, but that is a lesson for another day.

Learning What I Could Manage

Don't Ignore the Pause

When you feel a slight hesitation within yourself, take heed. Some people call it their Spidey-sense, their conscience, or divine intervention. How you identify it does not matter if you ignore it.

Once you are old enough to speak for yourself, the only person who can say no for you is you. The people you are trying to please or gain favor with will not have to live with the consequences.

Once you are old enough to speak for yourself, the only person who can say no for you is you.

I don't know if any of the other girls felt a hesitation the day of the water gun battle, but I did, and I ignored it. I was also the only one who spent weeks on crutches as a result of ignoring it. That day was not the last time I felt that pause, and I got better at listening and choosing accordingly.

Yes, people may get upset with you, but if the relationship is worth it, that person or those people will be able to withstand being told no. I once heard a school principal tell a group of parents that we don't really know each other until we disagree. Your no can reveal someone's character and motives. Are they still kind and respectful toward you, or do they suddenly treat you like gum on the bottom of their shoe? You will easily find out if someone really cares about you after you don't give them what they want. Their behavior and how long they stick around will serve as your answer.

Be a Duck

The customer who gave me a tongue-lashing on the phone that day not only taught me not to take things personally; he also taught me to be a duck. Every time I encountered a problematic person, I would say to myself, *Be a duck*, to remember the image of water rolling off a duck's back. This was my mental cue to let it go. I did not want to carry the stress, anxiety, or negativity of others.

After several reminders to myself to be a duck, I pretty much became one. I could easily transition from one ugly interaction to my next responsibility without carrying emotional weight. We don't have to allow a person's negative attitude to infect our positive disposition. There is no way to shield yourself from every mean, rude, or hateful person, but you can be like a duck: Let it roll off your back and carry on with your day.

We don't have to allow a person's negative attitude to infect our positive disposition.

Growth Reflection

Now it's your turn to look back at your own life stories and see what you've learned—or still need to learn. Were there any common threads in my stories that sparked a thought for you, or did a message resonate in a way that reminded you of experiences that have impacted your life?

Take a moment to answer the questions below and capture your thoughts while they are newly present in your mind. No experience is wasted when we learn. Let's start with saying yes.

In the Past: Was there a time when you said yes, and it turned out well? Was there a time when you said no, and it turned out well? What did you learn from those experiences?

In the Present: Are you missing opportunities to say no that could make space for vital yeses? Is there an unspoken no that could declutter your life and create capacity?

Thoughts

CHAPTER 2

NAME

Name: A word or set of words by which a person, animal, place, or thing is known, addressed, or referred to.

I GOT MARRIED WHEN I was eighteen years old. Depending on your worldview, you instinctively scowled, your eyes got bigger, or you didn't think much of it. Most of the people in my circle at the time had a visible reaction and politely fought back the look of shock. I get it. Before I was eighteen, if I had heard of someone getting married at an early age, I would have been taken aback as well. In fact, I did experience this, but we know the saying—you can never fully understand a person's journey until you walk in their shoes.

I remember being in physical education class at fifteen years old and some of the kids were whispering about a young lady in the class who had gotten married. I looked toward the other side of the gym where she stood near other kids, but not exactly with them. There were many students in the class, and she and I had never spoken to one another. I did not even know her name, but somehow as I stood there listening to others express their shock, I was just as curious as I was surprised. As much as I had been told as a kid to stay out of grown folks' business, she was my age, and I felt compelled to ask. I walked across the gym, introduced myself, and asked her if she was married.

We both stood there in our basic gym shorts and cotton T-shirts. Her answer was as simple as our attire—"Yes." She was sixteen, and she was not ashamed or embarrassed. It was an easy affirmative and perhaps the most matter-of-fact response I had heard from someone our age. I asked how. We were too young to legally get married. She said her parents had given consent for her to marry a young man in the military.

She was soft-spoken but not weak, and her tone was confident. I don't recall asking any questions after that, and it wasn't a lengthy encounter, but I admired her strength. I am sure she knew much of the chatter in the gym that day was about her new nuptials, but her posture never changed, and she carried on like it was a normal day. I never would have imagined that a little over three years later, I would be married too.

The look of shock on people's faces did not end when I was eighteen. It happened for years when it was my turn to answer the same question. (It still happens today.) I became careful with sharing my age and how long I had been married in the same conversation. I could see the wheels turning in people's minds as they did the math. Some were polite but clearly appalled. Others openly voiced their opinion. It took me several years to gain the matter-of-fact confidence that young lady modeled in phys ed class just a few years prior.

I had my own moment of shock just a few weeks after getting married. Have you ever experienced shock that impaired your senses? Shock that made you feel like you were in a big cinema battle scene, minus the danger? If you are fond of war movies like I am, you can picture it. It's the part of the movie where the blast goes off near the main character and he grabs his ears, squints his eyes, and is totally dazed for several minutes while he tries to regain control of his sight and hearing. All the sounds are muffled, and his vision is hazy. We know he is going to survive. He is the main character, for goodness' sake, but he needs a moment to recover. Though I wasn't in any danger the day I got an official birth certificate so I could update my Social Security card with my new name, the moment left me dazed and confused. I had already experienced that shocker moment a few years prior (more on that in the next chapter), so the feeling was familiar, and the effects wore off more quickly this time around.

I had been using a tattered paper with "Certificate of Birth" printed across the top for everything that required legal documentation. It was a photocopied version of an original, but nonetheless acceptable in every arena where it was presented—school registration, obtaining a driver's license—all the official rites of passage that led me to believe my document was legit.

However, I learned it was unacceptable the day I went to apply for a name change on my Social Security card. I was puzzled. I was informed that I would have to get an original copy of my birth certificate and the only way to do that was to request it from the records office in my birth state. Technology did not offer the conveniences of today back then, but fortunately I had a family member in town who welcomed my company on the ten-hour drive north, so I made the trek.

The line was a long, winding maze the day I arrived at the records office. I am not a fan of lines, and at the time there were no smartphones with apps to play games, listen to music, or read books. There was just good old-fashioned snail's pace patience. Thankfully, my travel buddy accompanied me to the office, so the length of the line gave us plenty of time to talk. A feeling of relief swept over me when I finally reached the counter. The lady who greeted me did not share my excitement. She was expressionless as I stood at her station.

I approached with a simple and bright, "Hello, I need to get a copy of my birth certificate so I can update my Social Security card." She only needed the first part of the request. It made no difference to her why I needed the birth certificate, and she stuck to the script with her reply.

"Name, please."

She made no eye contact as she sat in a counter-height chair. Her fingers stood ready to type, and as soon as I gave her my name, her fingers went to work searching the database.

"Date of birth."

She did not crack a smile. I don't remember the time, but she looked like she was ready for the day to be over. I told her my birth date, and the keyboard clacked again.

"Spell your name."

I spelled it for her, and her blank demeanor held steady. Then she informed me that there was no one in the system with that name born that year.

I am sure confusion was evident on my face. My tattered paper with the last name my mother and I shared that served as a birth certificate for so many years stated otherwise. I politely responded, "It must be there. I was born here and that's my name." I asked her to check the spelling of my name as I spelled it again.

She looked at me. Finally, eye contact. Then she asked, "What's your father's last name?"

I am not sure if confusion and bewilderment look much different on my face or any other face, but I shifted from the former to the latter. Her question made sense, but for me it felt like it came out of left field, so I informed her that I didn't share my father's last name and asked her to check the information she'd entered again. She looked at me and clearly communicated with her eyes, *Honey, I do this all day. I know how to type a name and date of birth.* It was one of those scolding motherly looks that speaks without speaking.

Then she asked again, "What's your father's last name?"

I dug in my heels. "I don't have my father's last name."

She dug in her heels with a flat, steady tone. "What's your father's last name?"

Neither of us raised our voice, and neither of us wanted to give in.

"Miss, I told you my name." Despite her making it clear that her computer would not, better yet, *could not* produce what I was asking for, I refused to relent. I pulled out the raggedy paper that served as a birth certificate until just a short time ago. She looked at it, unimpressed, and asked again.

"What's your father's last name?"

"I don't understand why you are asking my father's last name. I don't use my father's last name," I repeated. I told her my last name as she stared at me.

She was unfazed. Although she looked like she was ready for the day to be over when I first approached the counter, apparently, she had all day.

"What's your father's last name?"

Finally, in frustration, I blurted out my father's last name, and before I could finish explaining again that it was not my last name, her fingers, which I did not even realize were still standing at attention, began typing. Just as I began making my case one more time, she said, "Here you are." She found me in the database—my first name with my father's last name. I repeated the newly discovered legal name in my head and thought, *That's not me. That sounds strange. Those names don't go together.*

In the same breath she informed me of how much I needed to pay for the copy of my birth certificate. "What form of payment will you be using?"

My mind went blank. I thought, *Wait . . . what?! I'm still processing the name part.*

Someone could have smacked me across my face and created less shock. I worked hard to maintain my composure, but inside I was twisting and turning like a dinghy in an ocean storm. My limbs became heavy and frozen.

In the blink of an eye (more accurately, the stroke of a key), I discovered that the name I had used my whole life was not my own. I had no emotional connection to the name that legally was, and all of this was uncovered by a pending name change. I had never felt more in limbo than I did at that moment. Everyone who loved me knew me by the name that just washed away like an empty shell carried out by the tide. I thought about all the times I had signed what I thought was my name and how many keepsakes I had in a name that did not belong to me.

My travel buddy stood beside me, silent. Her face was soft and consoling as I looked at her, thinking, *All these years this wasn't my last name.* My mom and my sister had the same last name, and I didn't. Technically, I would not have had the same last name anymore anyway, because the whole purpose of this rendezvous was to get the official document to change it, but I felt like my identity had been stolen.

The clerk saw the shock on my face. I wanted to cry. I felt that glassy glaze forming on my eyes as I fought back the tears. I apologized for going back and forth with her. It all felt so unnecessary. Her posture shifted and she softened. She did not venture too far off script, but she understood the space I was in.

This was new territory for me, but not for her, obviously, which is why she knew to ask for my father's last name. I paid the money and walked toward the exit. My legs felt heavy and unsteady as I wrestled with my thoughts. How did this happen? Why did this happen? The rest of the day was a blur.

Learning What I Could Control

Ask Yourself, "What Am I Afraid of Losing?"

Power, identity, and affection are just a few of the things we hold on to. That transient moment where I no longer had the name I knew, did not connect with the one I was given, and had not officially changed to the new name tested my sense of self.

Many years ago, the show *Sesame Street* taught kids how to identify the thing that was different with the game "One of These Things (Is Not Like the Others)." Images of objects that were similar and one that was clearly not the same lit up the screen. Think of three kids dancing in blue shirts and one kid dancing in a red shirt while someone sang, "One of these things is not like the others. . . ." I was the red shirt. A red-shirt athlete sits out for a season, and I was sitting on the bench alone. I felt like an outsider when I thought about my mom and my sister having the same last name, but thankfully the feeling was only momentary.

Most high school students read Shakespeare's *Romeo and Juliet* and come across Juliet's famous line, "What's in a name? That which we call a rose, by any other name would smell as sweet." I quickly realized that the love I felt for and from everyone in my circle did not change because my name was different. My mom was still my mom. My sister was still my sister. My new husband was still my husband, and I loved and was loved by many others. Ruminating and stressing about something I could not control would keep me from moving forward peaceably with what was to come.

I had to let the emotions go. Losing something is not always negative. Sometimes we need that space for new and better things, or we just need the space. Clutter in the soul is worse than clutter in a house. My advice: Do not allow what you are afraid of losing to keep you from enjoying what's in front of you. We get to choose to live an amazing life, and while it's good to reflect on and learn from what's behind us, a life that flourishes can only be lived in one direction—forward.

Clutter in the soul is worse than clutter in a house.

Learning What I Could Influence

Don't Be Afraid to Ask Yourself, "What If I'm Wrong?"

Most people won't be wrong about their last name, but we're all wrong about something at some point. No one gets it 100 percent correct all the time, and if we are willing to see another person's point of view versus fighting to be right, we can save ourselves a lot of headache and even heartache. I could have told the clerk my father's last name the first time she asked, and looking back on that day with more mature eyes, I would have. If I believed that firmly that I was correct, what harm would have come from searching the name? The truth is my ego wanted to be right because I had no connection to my father's last name.

Ego and the need to be right will hurt personal and professional relationships. They will make us stubborn, and people will tolerate us but prefer not to be around us. Ego will save face before admitting to being wrong. Emotions get wrapped up in our fight to be right. Those emotions can be blinding, and the lack of sight (or foresight) will keep us from seeing what we may sacrifice in our quest to be correct. The antidote to ego is humility and being willing to admit when we are wrong. There is no harm in seeing another person's perspective. This does not mean we will adopt it, but we can civilly disagree.

The antidote to ego is humility and being willing to admit when we are wrong.

The next time someone does not cosign on your perspective, simply stay curious. Ask yourself, "What if I'm wrong? What if there is an alternative or a better option?" Think about their perspective and ask questions to learn more. You may learn that their idea is more effective or efficient. You may conclude that a collaboration of the ideas proves the sum is greater than individual parts.

Learning What I Could Manage

Of No Concern

My status of married at eighteen did not change the quality of life, day-to-day responsibilities, or otherwise general position in life of the people whose opinions and judgment I was trying to avoid. At first, I was proud and excited to share my married status with others. Then I learned not everyone shared my excitement. I was too worried about what people who had no bearing on my day-to-day thought about me. Keep in mind that I struggled with people-pleasing, so this started many years before I was married, and the judgment of others made it more pronounced.

I agree that our actions impact others, and I also agree that most actions are of no concern. That may not make sense the first time you read it, but this example may help. I think that capable adults should contribute to a productive society (this impacts others), but whether one decides to be a judge or a janitor is of no concern. Both are productive and contributing citizens.

Like I said, it took me years to muster the resolute strength that young woman exhibited in physical education class, but I also had to learn that most people are concerned with the day-to-day affairs of their own lives. They want to make sure that they can provide for their families, their kids are safe, and their comfort is not disrupted. Even if they did pass judgment, it was fleeting because they quickly returned to their responsibilities. My concern for that judgment needed to be fleeting as well.

I had not learned to be a duck yet, but everything in life is a stepping stone for the next growth phase.

Years later I learned a quote popularized by Eleanor Roosevelt: "Great minds discuss ideas, average minds discuss events, small minds discuss people." This was enlightening for me. Her wisdom made me realize I was putting too much emphasis on the people part—not talking about them but worrying about them. I had to elevate my thinking if I wanted to be among the great minds, and great minds create opportunities to elevate people.

Growth Reflection

In the Past: Is there something in your past that you have fought to be right about? What would be the benefit of considering other perspectives?

In the Present: Is there something you are afraid of losing—a relationship, identity, position, etc.? How does that fear influence how you navigate relationships and your ability to be honest with yourself and others?

Thoughts

CHAPTER 3

BASTARD

Bastard: A child born to parents
who are not married to each other.[2]

MY PARENTS WERE NEVER MARRIED . . . not to each other, anyway. Not even that common-law marriage where you live together for years and tell people you're married when you're really not. They've never lived in the same house. I've never lived with my dad. In fact, for half of my childhood, we didn't even live in the same state.

Many of the interactions with my father came courtesy of the mail carrier during those different-state years. My father would

---

2 *Merriam-Webster Dictionary*, s.v. "bastard," accessed July 29, 2025, https://www.merriam-webster.com/dictionary/bastard.

send my mom a handwritten letter with a check inside from time to time, usually around birthdays and holidays or before school started. I enjoyed watching her open the envelope, lay the check aside, and read the note each time his mail arrived. It felt like a family moment. For some reason, the days those letters landed in the mailbox were always perfect days. I only ever remember the sun shining and a blue sky. I felt brighter on the inside, too. A letter from him was an instant jolt of happy, and my mom always passed me the triple-folded paper immediately after she read it.

I didn't get to spend much time with my dad, so for me a part of him was in that letter. His handwriting felt confident, masculine, and deep like his voice. I knew he was real, but he was also tangible as I held the paper and read the note.

Our visits were usually in the summer, and I looked forward to seeing him that one time of the year when we made the trip back to New York. There were a few things that made summer official—the last day of school, a water gun fight, and seeing my dad. The time between the visits made the day I finally saw him feel like I was getting to connect with a beloved celebrity. The happiness of the letters did not compare to the joy I felt seeing him in person. There was always a hint of anxiety because truly we did not know each other well, not the way a daughter knows a dad who she eats breakfast with every morning and kisses good night every evening. My head felt like I was supposed to love him, but my heart wanted to love him. The discomfort did not temper my excitement. I always felt like a puppy wagging its tail.

CHAPTER 3: BASTARD

My twelfth summer would have been like any other, except it wasn't. My dad sent a letter well before the summer visit with a check inside. Its arrival was a bit off the normal schedule. Perhaps my mom needed help. I saw the letter in the mail, and as with all the letters before it, I bugged her to open and read it so I could have my turn reading it. I followed her up the dark wooden steps in our rented town house.

There was no break in my stride as I trailed her into her bedroom and sat beside her on the edge of the bed. I quietly waited for her to finish reading and pass the letter to me. The light from the window shone on her face, and the day was beautiful like every day before when his letters arrived. The sky was bright blue with wispy clouds. The green trees looked more vibrant against it. I smiled as she read. The sunlight that graced her face was not illuminating a smile. Her expression became more serious with each line. My smile faded. Her serious expression morphed to upset. Upset evolved to mad. She told me I could not read the letter.

"Hmm, why not?" I asked.

She stood up and tore the letter to tiny pieces and threw them in the small trash can as she walked out of her bedroom. I looked at her back as she walked away, and then I looked at the small wastebasket. I thought, *Oh no, she ripped up Daddy.*

Her not letting me read the letter made me want to read it even more. She held a night shift position at a nursing home, so I waited for her to go to work so I could get to work putting the letter together. Luckily, there wasn't much garbage in the trash can. I carefully removed every piece from the wastebasket and carried them to my room, cradled in my hands. I turned on my desk lamp and gently spread the pieces on the surface of my white laminate desktop. I attempted to put the puzzle together, but the pieces were too small and each edge was too frayed. I needed something to make them stick. *Vaseline!*

I grabbed the Vaseline from the bathroom and smeared it on my desk. I laid each piece on the glossy surface ever so gently. Unfortunately, the ink on the pieces of paper began to smear.

Hurry up or it will be a blur, I told myself. I knew I didn't have much time.

As the letter came together, I recognized that familiar handwriting. Finally, I could read it. The light from the lamp bounced off the Vaseline, creating a shiny glare. As my eyes moved from left to right, suddenly I was aware of the darkness outside. I had never read any of his letters at night. The trees outside the window made it feel even darker. My small desk lamp lit the now fuzzy words as I read.

He was stressed, he said.

This isn't the usual "How are my girls?" letter. The tone is off. Something is not right.

He didn't ask for any of this.

He didn't ask for what?

Too many people were asking him for money.

Why are people asking him for money?

He has to help . . . *I don't recognize that name.*

Wait, who is she? I don't recognize that name . . . or that one.

Who are these people? Why do they need money? Hold on . . . there are more bastards!

I was heartbroken. I never had any hope of my parents getting married or us being a family. My father was in a relationship, and I knew I was a bastard, but my sister and I being the only bastards made us special bastards. You know, like he slipped up because he and my mom created this unique, unethical, special, we-were-meant-to-be-but-can't-be bond. What my parents had was not like what he had with anyone else—was it? It was like someone selling you an exclusive one-of-a-kind special edition and then you see someone else with the same thing shortly after you leave the store.

Wait . . . this is not special. This is not unique. It's . . . ugh. Now I'm mad too.

I was also confused. The best and worst thing I could have done that day was read that greasy letter. It was like seeing a sight you can't unsee, and you're never the same once you've seen it.

He should have written this in a journal instead of sending it in the mail. Too late. I read it.

My heart was heavy the next morning, and it showed. I told my mom I read the letter. She was shocked, but a small smirk of pride for my perseverance tickled the corner of her lip when she learned that I smeared Vaseline on my desk and reassembled it like a puzzle. She scolded me for reading the letter after she trashed it, but the smirk had already won. I did not take the chastisement seriously. She told my dad I read it, and I didn't care.

All the celebrity luster had worn off the next time I saw him. If there was a puppy lingering inside me, its tail wasn't wagging. The letter was an unpleasant distant memory, and now he just looked like a man who was my father. I was not feeling the daddy vibes, and it was evident. The joyous luster of my greeting faded. The hugs were not as tight. It was all respectful protocol at that point. I was obedient, so when he said he wanted to take my sister and me for a ride, I got in the car. I sat quietly in the front passenger seat. His car was comfortable with big cushy seats. I always felt small in his car, like his little girl, but on that day, I felt like a stranger. He asked the usual questions about school and preteen life. I answered and tried to muster a smile, but it's hard to make your mouth do what your heart doesn't want to.

We drove to a part of town that was familiar, but I didn't know the street. He parked and then gave me instructions. I stood ready as he told me to go to a house about four doors down on the opposite side of the street, ring the doorbell, and ask for a woman whose name was not familiar to me. I didn't know whose door it was, and I didn't know who the woman was, but I did as I was told. I looked back at him before I rang the doorbell.

He was standing beside the driver side of the car; my sister still sat in the back seat. A woman opened the door and smiled when she saw me. I executed the request as ordered—perfect soldier. The woman's face hardened when I mentioned the name. I wondered what that was about. She looked past me to see my father standing by the car. I turned to look at him too. He didn't move. She turned and walked back into her house, so I turned

and ran back to the car. My father asked, "What did she say?"
"Nothing," I responded.

We waited for a few minutes, and then a young woman came out with a baby on her hip. I had seen enough mothers and babysitters carry a child to know that this was her baby. I thought, *This is interesting*. She walked toward us, smiling. She approached my father, and he gave her a hug and a kiss. He greeted the baby she was holding too. I was perplexed, and I had no idea who she was. Then he said, "Tori, I'd like to introduce you to your older sister. . . ."

The name did not match the woman I had just asked for. It only took a second for my heart to start racing. My mind was racing too. I stood frozen and thought, *WAIT! This is my what?* My memory quickly flashed back to the torn, glossy letter, and I remembered seeing her name. *The woman standing before me with a baby is my sister?*

It felt like someone had just hit me with a sledgehammer. My vision blurred. I couldn't see. I couldn't hear. I was present but I wasn't there. Their voices sounded far away and hazy; I needed to snap back to reality.

Suddenly, I became aware of my little sister. She had gotten out of the car and was standing beside me. My focus shifted to her. She was young, and she didn't understand. My thoughts kept racing as I tried to process what was happening and keep my attention on her.

Why do you look so happy?

Do you realize what is happening?

You're too young to know better.

Six-year-olds!

Stop wagging your tail.

The seeds of hurt, planted on the day I read that glossy, fragmented letter, took root that summer day and with time blossomed into full-grown disdain. For three years, I did not speak to my father. I did not care to read his letters when they arrived in the mail, and I did not want my mother to buy me anything with the money he sent. During our summer visits up north to spend time with my mother's family, I was intentionally distant around him. I wanted to stay as far away from him as I could when he came to our family home. I passed on the car rides, and if he planned an outing, I sat home and watched television. "No thank you" was my new favorite phrase. "Leave me alone" was the one that was clearly felt but never crossed my lips. In my mind, not only did I not need him, but I also was better off without him.

The days of distance climaxed during my fifteenth summer. The sun was setting as we got ready for the evening drive back down south. The customary goodbyes with family were underway, and as always, my dad came to the house for hugs and kisses to see his girls off. The car was packed, and if I could have gotten in that car without speaking to him, I would have. I knew I could not leave without at least the similitude of a hug; that would have been blatantly disrespectful. My hug was limp and half-hearted, and he capitalized on that moment. He'd had enough of me avoiding and distancing myself from him.

He lovingly held my arm, started walking in the direction of his car, and said he needed to talk to me. I did not want to talk to him, but part of me knew the conversation was overdue. I could feel anger and sadness rising with each step we took. My eyes started to well up. I worked so hard to stuff down those feelings and now they were betraying me, forming a lump in my throat. I couldn't speak if I wanted to.

We sat in the car as the sun slowly made its descent. I do not remember what he said, only how he looked—like he needed my help. He wanted to fix what was wrong, but he did not know how.

The lump in my throat exploded into tears and a fury of hurt. An emotional torrent, anger that made my chest heavy, and that overgrown plant from seeds sown three years ago were ripped up in that car. He endured the outburst that felt like a whirlwind consuming all the oxygen as I struggled to catch my breath.

When the dust settled, seeds of healing were planted where anger, bitterness, hurt, strife, and division had grown. It was not all perfect in that moment—seeds need time to germinate—but our connection was repaired, and the head that felt like it should love him and the heart that wanted to love him found their way back to each other. I felt relief. Tension that had been wrapping my heart like a sheath finally let go, and I did not even realize it was there. The weight of the anger lifted. It was the first time I had given him a real hug in years.

Dads Are Important

There was a time in our history when the word *bastard* simply meant a child born to unwed parents. The word has always had a negative connotation; however, there was a time when its use was more likely to state a fact than to hurl an insult. There is no point in history (that I am aware of) that it was good to be a bastard. Though "bastard" may be more accepted now than it has ever been, there was a time when it evoked shame. As an insult, it was hurled at anyone who annoyed, offended, or was generally disliked. Say something to someone that they do not like, and you may receive the rebuttal of "you bastard."

Substantial research has been done on the effects of children growing up without their father. I can quote myriad articles stating that children who grow up in a household without their biological dad are more likely to live in a home supported by government welfare programs, drop out of school, end up in poverty, join a gang, commit a crime, use drugs, need mental health treatment, and engage in or suffer from an array of other vices and unintended consequences. All you need to do is type "growing up without a father" into your favorite search engine, and you will get more resources than you care to read. For many, the effects linger into adulthood, and if the challenges did not manifest during the formative years, there is no doubt that growing up without a father in the house has a huge impact on the way one navigates the world as an adult, even if it is in the form of greater resilience.

I've heard mothers raising children on their own tell their

kids that they, the single mother, are the mother and father—but that's not possible. It may make the child feel better momentarily (and the mom may feel stronger for declaring it), but the void is still there. Kids need both parents, and one cannot replace the other.

First Leaders

Parents are a child's first model of leadership, and even poor models are beloved by their children. Unsavory behavior can be regarded as normal when you don't know any different. Several years ago, I volunteered at an orphanage. The property had multiple homes with houseparents (as they were called) caring for children of different ages and ethnicities. People in the community donated anything and everything a kid could want, including trips to Disney World. The children in the orphanage were gifted more toys and trips than many children in the same community who lived in two-parent homes had access to. They had everything they wanted except one thing: their parents. The director of the orphanage told me that many of the children came from abusive and drug-infested homes; however, they would rather be in a dysfunctional home with their parents than in the orphanage.

I cannot imagine the trauma of being taken from your home, changing schools, leaving your friends, and disconnecting from everything familiar, including your family, and moving to a new location with strangers. Granted, they were kind and loving strangers, but they were unfamiliar, and they weren't family. All the gifts and trips did not quell the longing to return home to their parents. The happy moments created in the new environment were circumstantial and short-lived, and although the orphanage was not attempting to erase the desire for home and parents, the minute the trip was over, so were the smiles. I conducted fitness classes with the children, and I can tell you that sad bodies don't like to move. Nothing brings comfort like Mom and Dad.

Some homes are dysfunctional, and some are healthy and nurturing; they're all occupied by humans—and humans are flawed. If you want to expose all your bad habits, have children. They will copy behaviors, repeat phrases, and model attitudes faster than anything else you can teach them. Why? Because parents are their first leaders. There's a tether that ties a child's heart to their parent, and more than any made-up character, Mom and Dad are their heroes (even when they reach an age where they're too cool to admit it).

Learning What I Could Influence

No One Likes to Be Blindsided

I learned a lot the day my father instructed me to knock on that door. The pain I felt from reading his letter was my own doing. My mother tried to protect me from that heartache, and looking back, I'd say he figured that I knew about the people in the letter, so then was as good a time as any to meet them. It took some time for the shock of that day to wear off.

No one likes to be blindsided, not even kids. Now, if that blind side comes with a cake, some ice cream, and people jumping out to yell "surprise," that is completely acceptable. However, generally speaking, being blindsided is a bad thing. Just ask any quarterback.

Pregaming is a courtesy. In some instances, it is not only a courtesy, it is a necessity. If you know what it feels like to be caught flat-footed in a meeting or taken aback as information comes to light that you were not privy to beforehand, you understand the importance of advance notice. The people impacted will thank you when you give them a heads-up. They will also respect you. It's not uncommon for pregaming to happen in a business setting, but we can do the same for our kids. They have feelings too, and we teach them how to treat others by how we treat them and how we interact with people inside and outside our home.

Now, if that blind side comes with a cake, some ice cream, and people jumping out to yell "surprise," that is completely acceptable.

Learning What I Could Manage

Stuffing Down Emotions Does Not Work

I am not a psychologist, but my observation is that nothing good comes from stuffing down our emotions deep inside. They must be released in a safe and constructive way, or they will find a way to come out on their own. The latter may be dangerous and destructive; however, pain can also be a motivator.

I have had the privilege of meeting a lot of people. I've met men who fight to be the best dad they can be because their dad wasn't around. I know women who did not grow up with their father and when the romantic connection to their child's father was over, they did everything in their power to make sure his parental connection was not severed. In some instances, the man was not the most agreeable or likable person. He may have even been openly abusive. Some moms still fight to keep their child connected to the father because for them, that dad is better than no dad.

I was in a lot of pain the day my father took my arm and said we needed to talk, but I could not see it. I never talked about what was bothering me, and if something triggered the pain, I would find a private space and hide my tears. I am thankful my father initiated the conversation that day. I am not sure how my life would have turned out if he hadn't. He thought he was doing a good thing the day he took my sister and me to meet our half-siblings. (Yes, there were more.) Like I said, I felt like I'd been hit with a sledgehammer, and that jarring feeling was a lot for my adolescent body to handle. I did not have the maturity to see his perspective, and maybe he did not have the emotional intelligence to see mine, but we both suffered. I stuffed down those emotions for three years before the healing began, and even then, it took several years for me to find peace.

Hard conversations are tough, but we grow from them, and when things are not right at home, they're not right anywhere else. My advice, whether it is a personal or professional relationship that is suffering because of an offense, is to have the conversation. Be patient and understand that the other person has a perspective as well. Be willing to understand their point of view and their intentions. You may not agree, but it will help foster understanding. Remember, it's okay to ask yourself, *What if I'm wrong?* Go a step further and be honest with yourself by asking, *What if I am even partly responsible for the tension?* The world, your world, will not end if you're wrong. It will just be a reminder that you are human, and that means you're in good company.

Extend Grace

Although we cannot control what happens to (or for) us, we can control our response. It is not easy to fight the initial reaction of the shock-and-awe moment, but everything after that is up to us. I was angry for years, and the pain hurt me. I did not have the maturity to forgive my dad sooner, but the problem with holding someone in an emotional prison is you must stay in that prison with them to keep them bound. Let them go so you can be free too. The person may not deserve forgiveness, but you deserve a better life, and you will not have it unless you forgive.

It helps when we remember that we are imperfect. Flaws remind us that we are human, and although my quirks may look and feel different than the next person's, they are flaws nonetheless, and they are a part of what makes me uniquely me. Your flaws and quirks make you uniquely you. In fact, one day you may decide that some of the things you were not fond of about yourself are not even flaws. They are simply a part of what makes you who you are.

. . . the problem with holding someone in an emotional prison is you must stay in that prison with them to keep them bound.

Extend grace to yourself and anyone who has hurt you. Some things cannot and will not change; the sooner we accept that and make peace, the better off we will be. As you know, I'm speaking from experience.

Growth Reflection

In the Past: Did you have an experience or life-changing moment that you choose not to talk about? If so, does it affect your mood or actions in a way that harms you or others?

In the Present: Is there a personal or professional relationship in need of repair? Can you extend grace to that person for their imperfections? (Can you extend grace to yourself?) What is the first step you can take to mend the rift?

Thoughts

CHAPTER 4

TRAGEDY

Tragedy: A very sad event or situation, especially one involving death or suffering.[3]

SATURDAY MORNINGS WERE SPECIAL WHEN I was a kid. There was no rush to get out the door in time for school, and a day full of outside play was the norm. But first came Saturday morning cartoons. Kids all over my community sat crisscross applesauce as animated characters lit up the television screens. The commercials were just as lively as the shows, and if you

3 *Cambridge Advanced Learner's Dictionary & Thesaurus*, s.v. "tragedy," accessed July 29, 2025, https://dictionary.cambridge.org/us/dictionary/english/tragedy.

were fortunate enough to open a new box of cereal on Saturday morning, you had all the time in the world to find the toy inside.

The best part of Saturdays was time with friends. I loved being outside, and there were plenty of other elementary-school-age kids to play with. We had the energy to play all day. I'm sure I slowed down at some point, but I do not remember taking a break even to eat lunch. Most of the time we played on the streets near our homes, and we enjoyed everything from jump rope to freeze tag. Our improvised sidewalk chalk (white landscaping rocks in any nearby yard, perfectly sized for a child's hand) was just what we needed to start a game of hopscotch. Occasionally an adult would upgrade our fun with a walk to a park. The closest park to my home was roughly half a mile, and it never seemed far because fun was always waiting on the other end of the trek.

A day full of play was the best, and I learned there were several unwritten rules as I ventured all over the neighborhood. One rule was not to go inside anyone's house that my family deemed off-limits or didn't know. Taking food or candy from strangers was an absolute no-no, and under no circumstances was I allowed to get in the car with anyone other than family or a close family friend. There were also gray areas. As a general rule, my friends and I had to be within a reasonable distance of our homes when the streetlights came on. Venturing farther away usually happened on a bicycle, but even then, there was an invisible perimeter that only extended a few blocks beyond the streets we lived on. It was never clearly defined, but I knew when I approached it. It usually meant seeing adults I did not recognize, kids I did not know from school, and stores that were not on my errand route.

All the kids in my neighborhood had to walk to school once we reached the third grade. My walk was almost three-quarters of a mile, and I never considered that far, but I knew better than to walk that far alone for anything other than the walk to school. The walk to the park was 100 percent okay if we were with an adult. Walking to the park without an adult but with other kids was in the gray zone, especially if there were busy streets to cross.

Another gray area was playing in the street. It was allowed, but not in high-traffic areas and preferably closer to the sidewalks. Jumping double Dutch was acceptable along the curb where cars parked, but if all the street parking was taken, we had to be extra vigilant, and we knew not to play too close to the corner. That was a blind spot.

Needless to say, I looked forward to Saturday mornings. It was the prime time of my week. One Saturday, I ventured outside to play and to my surprise, there wasn't a kid in sight. I don't know why the kid population was slim that day, but the weather was perfect, and we never wasted warm, sunny days.

After several minutes, I came upon a girl I occasionally played with. She was with her older brother and his friend. The four of us decided to make it a playdate. We were completely bored after a few rounds of hopscotch. There weren't enough kids to play freeze tag, and back then we never would have dreamed of spending a sunny day inside playing video games.

Those were reserved for rainy days or cold-weather holidays when family visited from out of town. We decided to go to the park. Her brother was only two or three years older than she and I were, but in our eight-year-old eyes, he was the big kid, so he led the way.

We walked to the end of my street, lined with row houses and mature trees. We were familiar with our wide-enough-for-two-cars blocks, but to get to the park, we had to cross a much wider and usually busier street. On a weekday, the bustling community was full of drivers hurrying to work and pedestrians waiting for city buses. On a Saturday morning, there wasn't much traffic at all.

We turned onto the sidewalk at the edge of the wide, busy street and walked toward the park. It was as expected for a Saturday, an occasional car but nothing like a weekday. Our spirits were as happy as the weather. It was a beautiful day. We laughed and joked as we made our way, and I felt quite mature being in the gray zone with my friends. We knew we had to cross the wide and unusually quiet street at some point, so we got as close to the park as we could before we devised a plan that would ensure the four of us made it safely to the other side. My friend's older brother decided he would go first, and once he was safely on the other side he would watch for cars and then tell us when to run. We would each sprint as fast as we could across the street when he gave the signal.

The plan was set. He looked both ways, confirmed the coast was clear, and then jetted. He made it to the other side in no time flat. Once he was safely across the street, he yelled to his friend that he was next. They both looked right and left, and my friend's big brother yelled, "GO!" That kid took off like a starter pistol had fired and he was racing for a gold medal. Within seconds he was on the other side of the street. The two of them looked smaller and the street seemed so wide. My friend was up next. We all looked both ways and the street was clear. He shouted to his sister, "GO!" She took off. I looked to the right as she started running, and it seemed as if out of nowhere a car appeared in the distance. It was so far away that it looked small, too far and too small to be a threat. I sighed, thinking, *She's safe*. She kept running, but suddenly the car got closer and closer, and the street seemed wider and wider. There were no other cars except that one, and it was heading in her direction dangerously fast. I watched her run, thinking, *Surely, she will make it*, but my heart started to race as the car got closer. My legs felt weak as her brother began yelling, "RUN FASTER, RUN!" She ran as fast as her legs could carry her, and just as she got within a few feet of her brother, the white sedan collided with her defenseless body.

She flew in an arc against the clear blue sky and somersaulted in what seemed like slow motion. I watched her limbs tumble through the air before she hit the ground and slid to a stop. I screamed. Fear raced through my body as she lay limp on the pavement. It felt surreal. I wanted her to move . . . a simple shift in her arm or leg as a sign of hope . . . but nothing. I felt helpless.

I turned and ran home as fast as I could, taking the same path we had just walked a few minutes before when we were laughing and playing. We had no idea how all our lives would change in only a few minutes.

My stomach felt queasy with every step, and I could not run home fast enough. My brain could not reconcile what my eyes had just seen. I knew I saw it, but it did not seem real. I made it home on autopilot because suddenly, somehow, I was at my front door. The shock had not worn off when I burst into the house, barely able to speak as I pleaded for help.

My mom was able to decipher my full-panic-mode request, and we hurried along the same route back toward the park. I could hear the sirens and the frenzy of the tragedy as we got closer to the scene. The ambulance was already there. We stood on the sidewalk for a few minutes, and I remember the devastation and brokenness on the older brother's face as he stood on the other side of the street. He was only a few feet from the same spot where he had yelled "go." Several neighbors stood by silently as the medical team lifted his sister, my friend, into the ambulance. I never saw her brother again after that day. I can't imagine how he must have felt. His little sister woke up that morning like every other Saturday and was gone before the sun set.

My friend's mother called my mom that evening to share that they were going to take her off life support. She was too far gone. At that point in my life, I had only known of older people dying. That Saturday taught me that death did not discriminate. My friend would not watch any more Saturday morning cartoons, play hopscotch or freeze tag with friends, or celebrate any more birthdays. She had her last sunny Saturday, and for the next several days everything felt dark.

You're Never the Same

Once you see something, you cannot unsee it. When you experience something like this, you remember it for the rest of your life. Life goes on, but the memory remains. I thought about my friend's mom, her dad, and her brother and how their lives were impacted the most. She never got to experience the moments I enjoyed as a teenager and young adult, and her family did not get to enjoy them with her. She missed their moments too. Her parents didn't only lose their daughter, they likely lost their grandchildren and their great-grandchildren. Part of their family's legacy died the day she did. There is no way to know how her life would have turned out, but all the promises it held were shattered on that day. When a life is lost, everything that life offered to the world is lost as well.

Highs and Lows Are a Part of Life

I've been told by multiple people that I don't get too high or too low (emotionally). I don't know if it is by nurture or by nature, but I do know that tragedies (and for me, hard lessons in general) make most problems feel small by comparison. Some would call them first-world problems.

In the book *Think Like a Monk*, Jay Shetty tells the tale of a man who encounters what most people would view as highs and lows in life, but he never approaches them as such.[4] He lives in a rural village, and one day his horse runs away. His neighbor tells him how unfortunate that must be for him, and his reply is essentially, "It is what it is." The horse returns home and brings a wild horse with it. That same neighbor tells him how great it must be to have the horse back with a bonus horse. His reply is the same: "It is what it is." The man's son attempts to train the wild horse. The horse bucks and breaks his son's leg. You guessed it. The neighbor tells him how awful it is, and by now you know how the man responds.

Shortly thereafter, the country goes to war and soldiers visit the village to draft young men. When they arrive at the man's home to collect his son, they find him with a broken leg. Here comes that neighbor again, and yes, he views the son's broken leg as a fortunate event because he is in no shape to fight a war.

Now, I was cucumber cool when I first heard this tale, but here I began to feel the emotions rise. I thought to myself, *Wow. Talk about good timing. He is not in danger of losing his son.* I was on board with the neighbor, but guess what the man's response was? You got it. He stuck to his "it is what it is" guns.

Admittedly, I am not on that man's level, but the tale resonated with me. For me, tragedy had a way of suddenly making the things I got upset over or complained about seem insignificant.

---

4 Jay Shetty, *Think Like a Monk: Train Your Mind for Peace and Purpose Every Day* (Simon & Schuster, 2020).

Most things in life are relative, and sure, there are deadlines and challenges, but in most of what is expected of us, no lives are lost. Perspective has a great deal of influence on what we feel in any circumstance. I like to think of gratitude as the anchor that steadies the ship, and perspective steers it in the right direction.

Learning What I Could Manage

Appreciation and Perspective

When we leave home, we expect to return at the end of the day; chances are we will, but it is not guaranteed. I learned early to appreciate each day. The tragedy of losing my friend so young, as well as many other experiences, taught me how fragile life truly is. I had to learn not to get upset about little things and to focus on what I could control.

We get to love the people we are blessed with even when they annoy or upset us. (I have to remind myself of this from time to time.) At the risk of sounding judgmental, I don't understand when people say, "My kids are getting on my nerves. I can't wait for them to move out." Maybe I've seen too many broken families and learned more hard lessons than some, but I want to keep the people I love close for as long as possible.

For several days after her death, I kept wishing my friend would have stopped running and let the car go by or that she had turned around and run back to me. We can't change the past, but we can learn from it. I learned how quickly things can change—forever. Never let a hard lesson or season in life pass without taking something of value with you. As you can see, this experience taught me a few things.

Never let a hard lesson or season in life pass without taking something of value with you.

Don't Let Fear Paralyze You

The first walk to that park after my friend was killed was an anxious one. I was with my mom, so I felt safe, but the images of what happened raced through my head. I never forgot her, but it became easier with each walk. Inside every hard, uncomfortable, or painful lesson is a pearl.

We've all had to deal with difficult people and difficult situations. Sometimes the friction presents itself in the moment, but there are times when we anticipate the challenge. We know it's coming, and it makes us anxious. The business deal you don't want to mess up, the hard conversation you need to have with someone you love, or that phone call you don't want to make—they are all real situations. But my experience has been that these situations were far worse in my mind than they were in real life. The anticipation was worse than the reality.

There is a movie quote that captures this sentiment: "Fear is not real. The only place that fear can exist is in our thoughts of the future. It is the product of our imagination, causing us to fear things that do not at present and may not ever exist. That is near insanity. Now do not misunderstand me—danger is real. But fear is a choice."[5]

Have you ever noticed how one person may be afraid of something, while another person is excited about it? Or how someone may worry and lose sleep over a matter that the next person would not give an ounce of energy to? Fear is based on perception. Facing fears and overcoming them builds confidence. Big fears are easy to recognize because they cause a visceral reaction, but the ones that rob our dreams and squelch our potential are harder to detect.

I was blessed with a real-world example to draw upon throughout life during a ninth-grade physical education class. The gym teacher instructed the class through a rotation of sports, one of which was the track-and-field skill of jumping hurdles. A few students at a time lined up to race as the gym teacher announced, "On your mark, get set, go!" I had never jumped a hurdle, and I was taken aback by the height. I ran toward the first hurdle, pumped the brakes, and stopped abruptly before running into what felt like a waist-high hindrance. My hands hit the metal, pushing

Big fears are easy to recognize because they cause a visceral reaction, but the ones that rob our dreams and squelch our potential are harder to detect.

---

5 *After Earth*, M. Night Shyamalan, director (Columbia Pictures, 2013).

the hurdle over before my legs came to a complete stop. I did not even try to clear the hurdle, but what stuck with me the most was the feeling as I approached it. It was similar to the feeling I got when I was younger right before I ripped off a Band-Aid. You know it is going to sting, but you know it needs to be done, so you do it. I became aware of the flinch that accompanied fear.

Recognition of the flinch, stopping short of the hurdle, helped me to identify fear. That awareness, or the hesitation it caused, is only the first step. The next step is doing it (whatever it is) anyway. Most people feel the flinch and procrastinate, busying themselves with something less important so they don't feel bad about avoiding the thing that needs to be done, while others make an excuse as to why it should not or cannot be done.

Worst of all is blaming someone else instead of owning the flinch. No one wants to say, "I am afraid. I flinched, and I don't want to push past it." That is too big a bruise to the ego, so we distract ourselves with other tasks and never get to the core of why we are not succeeding. We have to acknowledge the hurdle that caused us to flinch. Allow fear to paralyze you too many times and you will wake up one day unhappy, unhealthy, with unrealized potential, living an unsatisfactory life. Push past the flinch.

Growth Reflection

In the Past: Have you had an emotionally jarring experience? Did it make you better or limit your ability to thrive?

In the Present: Is there an area in your life where you flinch? How can you become more self-aware and identify what causes you to shrink back, stall, or avoid taking action?

Thoughts

CHAPTER 5

BULLY

Bully: A person who habitually seeks to harm or intimidate those whom they perceive as vulnerable.

MY MOTHER HAS ALWAYS BEEN infuriated by bullies. If you say "bully" to her, she gets fired up and tells the story of the girl roughly twice her size who bullied her almost every day. My grandmother had to keep buying schoolbooks because the bully was a pro at destroying them. As the story goes, the big bully girl approached my elementary-school-age mom like she did on all the other days with the aim of destroying those books. This time my mother knew she had to face the bully or face her mom. She chose facing the bully, and the bigger, more developed girl was left with her shirt torn open for all to see. That was the last time the girl bullied my mom.

I have had my fair share of attention from bullies, but I never understood what caused it. My mother said that as a kid I was tenderhearted, didn't bother anyone, and cried at the drop of a hat. I don't know if that made me a target, but she was right. I avoided conflict like the plague, and if I addressed it, it was only because I was fed up. Maybe I was too nice. But nice or not, somehow I earned the attention of a girl I'd never met. I became the focus of her hostility—it seemed—by simply walking past her house on the way to school. I did not know her, but she hurled insults at me every morning.

Her badgering was so frequent that it became background noise to me. You know that house in your neighborhood that has the yappy dog that barks at you each time you pass by on your leisurely stroll? Same you, same dog, same bark . . . different day. That was this girl. She never came out of the yard or tried to bite me, but she did a fair amount of barking. I wondered why she wasn't on her way to school too, but I just kept walking. No time to inquire, and in my mind, it was better to keep some distance between us.

One of my favorite pastimes as a kid was riding my bike around the neighborhood. One day I was riding in the alley behind her house, and she started barking back there, too. I had never seen her at the back of her home, but that day she was on guard. My patience wore thin with Yappy, and I wasn't feeling so tenderhearted, so I told her to shut up. She exploded and warned me that I was going to get it this time. Whatever "it" was, I wasn't worried about it because that pooch never left the porch.

On my next lap around the block, she was standing in the alley with a boy who looked like he could eat me for lunch. I hit the brakes and skidded to a safe distance. The narrow alley felt even smaller, with the fences from each backyard creating a makeshift wall and the two of them blocking the path. She stood in front of him wagging her finger and rolling her neck as she announced that he was her big brother. I didn't know she had a big brother. Where had this kid been hiding? Then she began barking that her brother was going to beat me up for telling her to shut up. He stood there, angry, and reaffirmed his sister's message. I couldn't believe he was really going to do it. This boy, who was considerably larger than me, was planning to help his sister beat me up, and all I'd said, after weeks of that yappy dog, was "shut up."

I could feel my heart racing, and it wasn't from the bike ride. I knew better than to argue or fight with either of them, so I told them I would be right back, and when I got back, we could settle it fair and square. I turned my bike back in the direction I had come from and rode as quickly as I could to a neighbor's house. I did not have a big brother, but I knew where I could borrow one.

There was a boy in our neighborhood who none of the kids messed with, but I was friends with his little sister, so he was always kind to me. He was the type of kid who we all figured would end up dead or in jail, and all the boys knew not to cross the line with him. He wasn't that big, and he was an attractive young man, but none of that mattered to him. He was fearless, and he would fight anyone.

I knocked on the door, panting, barely able to explain what was happening, but he was able to make out "big boy" and "beat me up." He said, "Show me where he is," and he started walking. In the blink of an eye, we traveled the two blocks over, and I couldn't believe they were still standing there waiting for me to come back. The yappy dog's big brother instantly recognized my borrowed big brother. I watched his posture change and his tail tuck under the moment he saw him. I was amazed. They were about the same age, but they were not the same size. If Yappy's big brother was a beefy future lineman, my borrowed big brother was a lean future wide receiver. I didn't know the story of David and Goliath back then, but this Goliath knew how the story ended. He wanted nothing to do with my David. Suddenly the lineman began to giggle and said, "We were just playing with her. We didn't mean it."

I was appalled.

"What!" I said. "No, you were not. You threatened to beat me up."

He did not waver from his reasoning and made sure my borrowed big brother knew he did not want any trouble. He even quieted his little sister. From that day forward, that dog never barked at me again.

It would be a few years before I encountered another bully. This time I was the new kid at school. I didn't have a borrowed big brother, and this bully came with a pack. Middle school is a challenging time for some kids. It was for me because a girl twice my size made me her target and brought four pint-size friends along for the ride. They said mean things when our paths crossed in the hallway, slipped hateful notes in my locker, gave me dirty looks in class, and tried to get laughs at my expense. At first my strategy was the same as with Yappy: Ignore them. And I did until I couldn't.

One day I stopped to get a sip of water at the fountain. One of the pint-size pack members came uncomfortably close, breaking all personal-space rules. She told me to move so she could get some water. I ignored her. She repeated herself and added colorful language. I stopped drinking, lifted my head, calmly told her she would have to wait her turn, and continued to drink from the fountain. I remember thinking, *This girl could knock me in the back of my head right now*, but I was fed up, and I did not want her to think I was afraid of her or her bully friends. Just like Yappy, she exploded. She began to make a scene, yelling, "She talks! Oh, she can talk! You're going to get it now! Wait until after class!"

I loved school. Learning was and still is my happy place, so I forgot about her threat until I walked out of the classroom and momma bear plus the four baby bears were all waiting for me. I could not appreciate it then, but I should have been impressed by the diversity of that group. Almost every shade of people on God's green earth was in that bully pack, but none of that mattered in that moment. I only made it a few feet from the classroom door when the pack flanked, causing me to move backward and confining me between two sets of lockers. The water fountain where the pack member made her promise was still in view. My back was against the wall across from two classrooms, and for years I wondered how the teachers did not hear all the commotion. A group of bystanders surrounded the pack, creating a semicircle that made an easy escape impossible; they wanted a fight. I still had my backpack on, and I felt it pressing against the wall. The bully pack was spewing within inches of my face, and I knew if I pushed forward to escape, it would only hasten them putting their hands on me. There was a lot of noise, but my thoughts were calm and quiet. When I realized I could not escape, I told myself, *Today, you have to fight.*

I slowly lifted my right hand to grab the strap on my shoulder. I knew it would be harder to fight with the backpack on. As I slowly began to slide the strap, my head shifted slightly, and I was able to see through a narrow break in the mini mob. A male figure was walking toward the pack. I recognized him. It was the assistant principal. I calmly reset my right strap, stood still, and waited. I watched as the outer band scattered with his approach. The bully pack was so fixated on me and yelling threats that they did not realize their audience had dissipated. I shifted my eyes from the pack to him as he stood sternly behind them, and there was no need to explain what was happening. He was witnessing it firsthand. My mother had already warned the school that I was being bullied, but momma bear and her crew kept denying it, even with a hateful letter and an administrator recognizing her handwriting as evidence.

Momma bear and I followed him to his office. We sat down

and he informed her that she'd been caught red-handed, and now he knew the bullying was true.

She giggled. "Bullying? No one is bullying her. We were just playing with her." This was familiar and unoriginal. I was not impressed, but then she crossed the line.

"I was only playing with her. We're friends."

"What?! Friends?!" I exploded. "You have been bullying me since the day I got here. I don't even know you. We are not friends."

Momma bear got suspended. She piped up a little when she returned to school, but the passion of the pack was gone, and she had no followers. The pack dispersed, and I cannot remember her speaking to me the rest of the year. One of the pack members did approach me to foster a friendship, but I passed on that opportunity. Momma bear still had her bully ways, but they seemed less effective without an entourage, and one day her methods were completely nullified by one kid.

There was a boy in our grade who piqued my curiosity. I only had one class with him, and he got in trouble more than all the kids in all my classes put together. He was labeled our resident rebel and a generally bad kid, but I remember talking to him a few times, and he had a warm soul. It was like watching pain personified when he misbehaved, and I felt awful for the teachers because I knew he made it hard for them. I did not understand why he was so rebellious and disrespectful to authority. He could be quite scary. He was one of those kids whose name you never forgot.

I felt like I swallowed a frog the day he quieted momma bear. The hall was bustling with students racing to their lockers and trying to catch up with friends before the bell rang for the next class. I stood at my locker gathering my books when through the sea of voices, I heard momma bear's voice drowning out the others. I turned my head over my left shoulder; my right hand was still on the locker door as I tried to narrow in on her location. Her voice was far enough away that I knew I was not the target. I realized in that moment that as much as momma bear had terrorized me, I had never heard her raise her voice in that way. She was yelling at our resident rebel.

The hallway was dimly lit except for one area where windows allowed natural light to brighten the gray floors and cream walls. They stood in the darkest part of the hallway far from the sunlight, but it was as if a spotlight was on them in that moment. She was bigger than him, but he did not care. He yelled back at her. They were in a yelling match when suddenly his right hand crossed her face so fast and hard that the sound turned every student in that hallway into a mannequin, including me. I couldn't believe what I had just seen. The most rebellious kid in school had just slapped the biggest bully in school—hard. My brain was flooded with thoughts.

He just slapped a girl.

He slapped her hard.

Don't hit him, momma bear. He will beat you up.

Momma bear stood still. She was a mannequin too. Her hand covered the side of her face as he stared at her, daring her to touch him. The shock began to wear off as students slowly started to move, but the hallway was quiet. Momma bear turned enough for me to see her fighting back tears behind her glasses. She had never looked more human to me than she did in that moment. Our resident rebel was expelled, and momma bear never bullied another kid again.

Bully Lessons

I am no expert on bullies, but my experience is that bullies feel they have an advantage over those they harass. For Yappy, it was a big brother, and in the case of my middle school encounter, it was size and the pack. For some it is money, power, or proxy power. Bullying looks different in adulthood, but regardless of how it manifests, there is a power or perceived power imbalance.

I learned something about myself from my bully experiences. I had a phase where I was reluctant to excel or appear too good at anything for fear of drawing negative attention. When you are granted bullies for simply walking to school or walking into a school, you try to fly under the radar. Thankfully, that phase was short-lived.

I woke up one day with a new mindset. I am sure it was more gradual than it felt, but I was tired of suppressing my authentic self. I had several positive people between home and school who encouraged me to be my best. As an adult I learned to ask, *Is the problem with me or with them?* Arguably both. It was my problem because I was dampening my growth and success by not going too far off par from others. It was their problem for not seeing the greatness within themselves and lacking the confidence to celebrate or see others succeed. This graduated to other lessons for me, such as don't be afraid when your circle changes, and new lessons require different teachers. The kindergarten teacher does not teach calculus, and they're not supposed to. You must elevate your circle and your teachers to elevate your life.

Bullies also taught me that I was tougher than I thought. I never sought conflict, but I did not back down when I was backed into a corner. I also learned that some people have your back without question, and sometimes we must call in reinforcements. When I showed up at the door of my borrowed big brother, he started walking even before I could fully explain the situation.

That leads me to my next lesson—no matter how big or powerful we get, there is always someone bigger or more powerful. The boy who planned to help his sister beat me up was quieted by my borrowed big brother, and momma bear was nullified by an even angrier and more rebellious kid. I was surprised that I felt even an ounce of compassion for momma bear. I thought, *Good riddance,* the moment that kid's hand crossed her face, and then almost immediately after, I felt sorry for her. She looked like a regular girl, not a big, mean bully. Her vulnerability was exposed; she was human just like the rest of us.

Learning What I Could Control

You Can Only Control You

I am sure the bullies had a reason to torment me that made sense to them. As much as I wanted peace from their antics, the only person I could truly control was me. I recognize that people can make it hard to be patient, be kind, and not lose our temper, but at the end of the day we own our actions. No one can make us curse, yell, or fight if we don't want to. The challenge is that the milliseconds between their action and our reaction may feel insufficient to assess the spark that lit the flame. That spark may be an insult, a threat, or whatever causes you to feel inflamed.

This is a good time to practice a pause to determine if the spark is worth igniting the fire. It is true that violence begets violence, and once the violence starts, it is hard to stop. Don't be afraid to take the high road; it's the harder path, and it requires more strength to climb.

The people who dislike you may never like you, but they will respect you if you don't match their behavior. Mark Twain is often credited with a couple of quotes that put a smile on my face. The first is "Never argue with a fool; onlookers may not be able to tell the difference." Another is "Never argue with stupid people; they will drag you down to their level and beat you with experience."

Don't be afraid to take the high road; it's the harder path, and it requires more strength to climb.

Who can argue with that? Take the high road and you will have honor in the midst of your adversaries.

Speaking of adversaries, if you are familiar with the story of Moses, you know that he had a big and powerful adversary.[6] Moses announced ten plagues against the land of Egypt, and all of them came to pass. This had to have made everyone who lived there miserable. Imagine that you live in Egypt during ancient times, and a man keeps coming to the leader of your country to tell him that awful things are going to happen if he doesn't stop being a big, bad bully. You have zero authority, and you have no influence over the leader, so you don't get to say, "Hey, can we just give this guy what he wants so he stops coming here making life hard for everyone? I'm just trying to work and raise my kids. Can you all please end this nonsense?!" Maybe you want to go a step further and say, "What is the problem? Can't we just get rid of this Moses guy? Someone take him around back and teach him a lesson."

It's a little-known fact that Pharaoh's servants and the Egyptians thought highly of Moses.[7] They thought he was a great man. Imagine that?

---

6 See Exodus in the Old Testament of the Bible.

7 Exodus 11:3.

Learning What I Could Influence

You Get What You Tolerate

You've probably seen over the years that an institution that tolerates bad behavior will inevitably get more of it. Every organization has a culture, and within that culture are subcultures that either support or detract from the overall culture, mission, and vision.

The simplest form of an organization is a family. I know; organization seems too formal to describe a family, but go along with me for a moment. If the people who are part of a family are corrupt, upstanding, rebellious, or productive, those people will impact their community. The community will impact the city. The city will in turn impact the state, and eventually the nation, which will influence the world. It may take decades to see the effects of the desirable or undesirable changes in culture, but they will manifest.

A business is similar. A rogue manager or team can infect a department and, if left unchecked, can wreak havoc on the company. Not all infections are bad. Fan the flame by celebrating and encouraging culture-affirming actions, such as sharing, collaboration, and skill-building, and you will get more of them. Acts as simple as a smile are infectious, and even kindness is contagious. These are easy to spread. I've heard leaders say

> **Fan the flame by celebrating and encouraging culture-affirming actions . . . and you will get more of them.**

you get what you incentivize. I'll add—incent what you want to implement. Part of a leader's obligation is to reward the right behaviors and avoid sending conflicting messages.

A *Forbes* write-up titled "Your Culture Is Defined by the Worst Behavior You Tolerate" describes the challenges of toxic behavior and its impact in the professional arena. The fallout usually includes turnover, absenteeism, and low productivity.[8]

I would argue that it looks similar in school. One advantage in the business world is that when things are going badly at work, employees can change jobs. But when things were going badly for me with momma bear and her pack, I could not change schools. As much as I loved learning, there were days that I did not look forward to being in the school building, because I knew I had to deal with those bullies. Thankfully, I had a parent who was willing to fight for me, but even with evidence, the bullying situation occurred for too long. The bullies kept getting away with bullying, so nothing changed. I am thankful the assistant principal walked down the hall on that climactic day or that story might not have ended as peaceably.

What I perceived as mental strength—ignoring the bullies and taking the punches—looked to them like passivity. The bullies did not see strength; they saw a punching bag and just kept jabbing.

We teach people how to treat us, and we define what is

---

8 Shannon Gabriel, "Your Culture Is Defined by the Worst Behavior You Tolerate," Forbes Human Resources Council, February 21, 2024.

acceptable by what we tolerate. After my mother spoke to the school administration and no action was taken, the bullying intensified, and the occasional "Are you going to tell your mom?" was added to their menu of taunts. Ignoring them did not work.

Our lesson as leaders (and we are all leaders in some regard) is to address bad behavior early. If one person, especially one with influence, is allowed to treat others poorly, skirt the standards, or commit undesirable acts without consequence, others will be inspired to follow suit, and it is more complicated to rein in fifty bad actors than five.

Growth Reflection

In the Past: Was there a time when you were ostracized or intimidated by the actions of another person? What did you learn from the experience, especially about yourself?

In the Present: Is there someone in your life who would appreciate you speaking up for them? Do you need to speak up for yourself? Perhaps you are the person causing angst. How can you become self-aware of your impact on others?

Thoughts

CHAPTER 6

LOVE

Love: An intense feeling of deep affection.

THE FIRST PERSON WHO I CAN RECALL being the object of my affection was my sister. The popular Kid Sister doll was one of my favorite toys, but everything changed when, at age five, I got a real kid sister. I loved my entire family, but I loved on her. There was no shortage of affection in our household, and extended family was equally loving, but I felt a different type of love for my sister. She was the cutest baby I had ever seen, and I felt like it was my duty to protect her. She was a fun-loving, adventurous kid from day one, and she did not make the protecting part easy.

You may have gathered that parks were hubs for fun in the

community where I grew up. Most days there were kids playing on jungle gyms, teetering up and down on seesaws, and spinning on the merry-go-round until the sky twirled when we stood still. It was a safe place to run free with friends without worrying about being hit by a car. The big kids and active adults tested their skills at the handball courts or with a game of pickup basketball. Occasionally, I would sit along the fence with my knees tucked close to my chest to watch my uncle run up and down the court for an action-packed game of five on five—no blood, no foul.

One early summer day my mother took my sister and me to a park near my elementary school. There weren't many kids at the park, and I remember feeling relieved because keeping up with a squirrelly toddler in a sea of little people was challenging. Some of the parks were better suited for big kids and others were better suited for younger children. This one was perfect for smaller kids. Of all the things we could do at the park, swinging was my favorite. I picked up my sister, put her in the high-chair-type swing, and began to push the back of the seat, gently propelling her forward. My mom perched on a nearby bench where she could see us. The swings were metal and blocky back then. The chains were metal, and even the slender bar that secured my sister in the seat was metal. The big-kid swings to the left of us were made of one rectangular block of metal, almost like a plank of wood, and each swing had the same matching metal chains tethering them to the frame. The seats were brutal in the heat, and we knew to make sure our shorts covered the backs of our legs on a hot summer day.

The big-kid swings were my favorite. A few pumps of your legs, and you felt like you were flying. A couple of years earlier, one of my older cousins taught me how to swing high and fast. She was fearless and loved to test the waters in everything. She gave me a master class on swinging high. She sat on the swing and helped me climb onto her lap so she and I could sit face to face with my legs straddling her. We must have been a sight to behold on that metal plank. She started by swinging low and slow. My weight added to hers meant more to move, but in no time, we were testing the arc and strength of the chains. She swung so high that for a brief moment we suspended gravity, achieving that floating feeling that creates butterflies in your stomach. As soon as gravity reclaimed our weight, there was an unnerving yank as the tension reengaged between the chains and the plank. The sound made me think we were going to snap the metal links and fly over the fence. I felt like I was on a roller coaster without the safety harness and begged her to stop. But she laughed and kept going.

When she finally realized that I was actually scared, she slowed down and stopped. I could not untangle my legs and dismount fast enough. She smiled, gave me a quick pat to reassure me all was well, and went back to playing as if she had not just scared the living daylights out of me. Experience taught her that we would be fine high up in the sky with our ponytails flapping in the wind, and I quickly dusted myself off and ran after her. That day she made me feel brave enough to swing high by myself.

The challenge with swinging high, however, was having time to react if a kid ran in front of you. Some kids made a game of darting in front of the swings, testing their luck by getting the timing just right. I never tested the waters in that way, but I had to be ready to test the rubber on my shoes if a kid unexpectedly ran in front of my swing.

I was glad no one was on the big-kid swings the day my mom took my little sister and me to the park, and the other toddler swings were empty too. It was just the two of us on that warm sunny day.

After a few minutes of pushing my little sister's swing, I spotted a girl I knew walking toward us. We'd been in the same second-grade class before the summer break. I annoyed her because I followed the rules, and she annoyed me because she didn't.

She was headed for the swings. I remember the feeling of irritation creeping over me as she got closer. She and I were definitely big-kid-swing size, but she chose a toddler swing. I thought to myself, *This is so like her.* There was no way she could sit in a toddler swing. Our legs were too big for the high-chair-type opening, so instead she stood in the blocky seat and started the pumping motion that was so familiar. She was taller than most of the girls in the class, including me, and she looked like a giant so high off the ground. I kept thinking to myself, *Why are you in that baby swing? Move over a couple of swings and get on the big-kid swings*, but neither of us spoke to one another. Standing up on the swings and going high was next level, and advanced swingers loved it. I loved it, but that was the first time I had seen anyone try it on the toddler swings. It was a ton of fun, but there was no testing the rubber on your shoes if someone ran in front of you. Some kids would go high and then bail, jumping and taking flight for just a moment before landing on the rubbery padded surface.

It could have been my distracted irritation with the girl beside us swinging higher and higher, or maybe my little sister had had enough and wanted to do something else. Either way, she got fussy and wanted to be done. I was careful to get her off the swing and usher her in the opposite direction toward the safety zone. We began walking toward my mom, when suddenly my sister ran back in the direction of the girl swinging high on that toddler swing. I turned to chase my sister but could not get there fast enough.

I knew what would happen next, but I was helpless to stop it.

The metal swing connected with my sister's head, and all the energy of that swing tossed her little body across the rubbery mats meant to keep kids safe. I ran to her immediately, and my mom was there just as quickly to grab her. The girl quickly dismounted the swing and ran to see if my sister was okay too. I remember a burning inside me that made me want to hit that girl, but I didn't—and that was not the priority. The priority was making sure my sister was okay.

There was a police precinct right beside the park, and my mother ran to it with my sister in her arms. I ran close behind, holding her purse.

Those little legs that had just been flailing with joy were now bouncing lifelessly with every stride my mother took. We entered the station in a panic. My sister was limp in my mother's arms as my mom pleaded for someone to call an ambulance. The officers gave us ice for the now growing lump on my sister's head, and my mother fought to keep her conscious. I vividly remember my mother saying, "We can't let her go to sleep." She tried to keep my sister's eyes open as she drifted in and out of consciousness. I was afraid. When my mother said we had to keep her awake, I reasoned that we had to keep her awake to keep her from dying. The thought of her dying scared me even more. Seeing her lie there with her eyes drifting sent my heart racing. Most days, she was full of energy and could barely sit still. On that day, I just wanted her to move.

The ambulance arrived within minutes. I had heard plenty of ambulance sirens before that day. They were background music, one of the frequent sounds that colored the soundtrack of city dwelling. When the ambulance arrived on that summer day, it was a featured track and deeply personal. I found solace in those sirens, and I was so happy to see the medics. The anxiousness I was feeling eased.

Fortunately, my sister recovered. After a few days the lump on her head receded and she was back to her fun-loving self. But we were in for some big changes. It wasn't too long after that day that my mom, my sister, and I moved from New York to North Carolina. Protective big-sister mode became more pronounced, and I felt even more responsible for taking care of her. Most of our family was within a few minutes' drive before the move, but suddenly the immediate warmth of the family circle was gone.

I can't say for certain if the bond between me and my sister grew stronger because the circle got smaller or if it would have regardless. I am inclined to believe that the move had a positive impact on our relationship. She had cousins closer to her age who would have been playmates and so did I, but in their absence, we became each other's natural companions. Oftentimes, my sister and I were home alone while our mom worked, and it gave us plenty of time to make good memories. We have a lot of stories from those days. We even made TV time fun by turning the coffee table into bunkbeds.

She and I laugh about it now, but I tried to convince her that her real parents were aliens, and we'd taken her in to care for her because they'd left earth. Yes, I know that was a cruel joke to play on a four-year-old and definitely not protective big-sister behavior. Coincidentally, my mom said her siblings played a similar prank on her. I'm not sure what motivated them, but I was motivated by one thing—my sister's adorableness. As I said, she was so cute, and her cry face was even cuter than her everyday life-is-good face.

As I tried to convince her of her alien family, her big brown eyes revealed that her brain was processing the idea. First, she had a look of concern at the first mention of her outer-space parents, and she said, "No they're not," but her rebuttal lacked confidence because she thought I might be telling the truth. Then I doubled down. Her bottom lip curled and started to quiver. The big brown eyes became adorable puppy-dog eyes and welled up with the first hint of tears. Her little face crinkled with sadness as she gave in to the tale. Maximum cuteness achieved! Just before she transitioned to full cry mode, I swooped in and reassured her that we were real blood sisters and that her parents were not aliens. The look of relief on her face was just as cute as her sad face.

I only got away with this trick twice, and the second time took much more convincing. By the third attempt, she brushed me off and suggested we get back to our regularly scheduled program because she was not falling for it anymore.

Big-sister mode continued when she started school, when she dated, and even when she got married. Although it was evident that she was a fully grown woman, one day I realized that it was time to let go; she was an adult. I don't think she felt the shift. More than anything, it was a shift in my own mindset. Of course, no matter how much she accomplishes in life or how old we get, there is still a warmth in my heart that feels like that childlike love every time I see her.

Learning What I Could Control

New Experiences Can Be Scary

I am grateful for every person who has ever pushed me out of my comfort zone. The push has not always been intentional or benevolent, but I learned that growth happens in discomfort. If we are willing to push past the discomfort, we might find that we enjoy the challenge and may even succeed at that new, once scary thing. Swinging high taught me this lesson. I was scared—very scared—but my braver older cousin taught me that it is okay to take risks. She also taught me to try new things. Her final lesson on that day was to shake it off. I am almost certain that her brief pat to console me before she ran off was simply her way of making the most of our limited time at the park, but I realized I did not have time to sulk. I had to make the most of my time too, and I did not want to waste it moping.

This is very easy to forget as an adult. Somewhere on the path to adulthood the fear of asking a silly question, losing, or appearing foolish dampens our willingness to take risks. You've probably heard the saying "Do it afraid." Most of us are simply afraid to do "it," whatever "it" is. Comfort and growth cannot reside in the same room. When one enters, the other must leave. Comfort only steps out momentarily, grabs a snack, and takes a walk. Whether that is a long or short walk depends on our response to the challenge, because as soon as growth completes its work, comfort walks back in the room and takes a seat. Now that comfort is back, growth makes its exit and may be gone for years unless we actively welcome it back.

New experiences can be scary, but they can also enrich our lives. Some of my best life experiences were on the other side of taking a risk, and so were some of my biggest lessons. Nelson Mandela said, "I never lose. I

Comfort and growth cannot reside in the same room.

either win or learn." As I grew older, I learned that I should not wait for people to push me out of my comfort zone. I should proactively seek discomfort because when I did, growth came more quickly.

Learning What I Could Influence

Trust Wins

The love between my sister and me was so strong that my alien-parents prank did not erode her trust. The time we spent together and the bond we built helped our connection withstand my antics. I showered her with affection immediately after the two times I was able to convince her, but she easily could have questioned anything else I told her from that point forward. She didn't. She knew how much I loved her, and she knew she could trust me.

I lacked the wisdom to consider the ramifications of my actions at the time, but she taught me that there is grace when we mess up if we have built enough trust to overcome shortcomings. She also taught me the importance and necessity of apologizing if we are wrong. Imagine if instead of showering her with affection and reminding her that I loved her, I said, "I was only joking; get over it." We are never too big to apologize. Our willingness to admit we are wrong is a way to show others that we care and that our ego is not more important than their feelings. This also builds trust.

Learning What I Could Manage

Be Ready for Anything

The day my sister was slung across the mat was a shocker. It taught me at a young age to be ready for anything and, most of all, that panicking does not help. The energy used to panic is put to better use with problem-solving.

I have facilitated many meetings with business owners. Oftentimes, we planned for outcomes regarding people, production, and revenue, focusing on their intended results. We discussed what they could control—leading indicators, team capacity, etc. One of my favorite parts of the discussion was planning for what had the potential to derail their plans. We brainstormed anything and everything—power outages, software outages, illnesses, phone service disruptions, building damage, a tight market . . . you name it. If you can think of it, we came up with it and formulated a way to mitigate each challenge. The only thing we did not include on the list or plan for happened—a pandemic. It was a reminder to be ready for anything.

This Too Shall Pass

All I wanted the day my sister got hurt was for her to get back to normal. Watching someone you love suffer is a hard pill to swallow. Now that I am a mom, I have experienced it in a different capacity. If someone you care about has been injured, been ill, or suffered in any way, you know exactly how I felt that day in the park. The heartstrings are pulled in an unexplainable way when you don't have the power to fix things. Fortunately, people are resilient. Just a few days after the scary head injury, my sister was sitting on the couch having a normal day—a stark contrast to the day that created so much worry. She was still as cute as ever, even with the big knot on her forehead, and I was thankful that I still had my sister.

Her recovery taught me a simple but valuable lesson—this too shall pass. Things may not play out the way we planned or hoped, but eventually the dust settles, and we can choose to thrive on the other side. You may not get the job or opportunity you wanted, but there are other jobs and there will be more opportunities. Continue to grow and you will be ready for the next time. Maybe the person you love didn't love you back, but there is someone in the world who will reciprocate your devotion, and you'll be thankful for the affection shared between you. Perhaps you didn't get into that school or you didn't land the deal. Maybe you "flinched" when you wish you had gone for it, and now you ruminate with regret.

If you are struggling to get past the disappointment, I have good news for you. Disappointment is a part of life. Very few things on this earth are permanent, and I confidently believe that if the door did not open, it was not meant for you at that time. A better option is on the way. Challenges bring out the best in us if we allow them—physically, emotionally, and spiritually. Most people do not welcome the pain of disappointment, but it reminds us that we are human, and we can thrive in spite of it.

Many years later, I learned that disappointment could reveal true desire. Losing or not getting what we want reveals how badly we want it and if we even want it at all. Olympians are a great example of this. Think about the athlete who trains for years, makes multiple sacrifices, and narrowly misses competing for a medal. I love a good comeback story. I admire those athletes who remained disciplined and trained for four more years just for the chance to compete again. It's even more rewarding when they take their place on the podium. Personally, I learned that if disappointment sharpened my focus, that was a clear indicator that I was all in.

Personal Life Impairs or Enhances Professional Life

It is hard to focus on work if we are worried about home. It is no surprise that our personal life impacts our professional life. This applies to children as well. Their schoolwork or social life may suffer if they have personal or home challenges. As adults, we like to think that we are good at compartmentalizing work and home. My personal experience and time supporting other leaders tell me this is not true. If someone has great relationships at home, it is much easier for them to thrive at work. On the contrary, when there is strife with a significant other or one of our children is struggling, our work may be gravely impacted. I have seen businesses derailed by challenges at home that took years to recover from, if at all.

When someone you love is not whole, the reality is that you

When someone you love is not whole, the reality is that you are not either.

are not either. Our emotional health is tied to their well-being, and rightfully so. Remember the section about being ready for anything? Life is unpredictable, and sometimes the people closest to us are a part of that equation. My mind could not rest until I knew my sister was okay.

We cannot always control what happens to us or the people we love, but most people do not consider the importance of readiness in advance. Think of it like insurance; you must have it in place before you need it. Most things that help mitigate hard times require investing and take time to build. A loving support system, a cushion of resources, and, in some cases, a strong personal and professional network can help soften the blow. The importance of strong faith and a positive mindset cannot be understated when dealing with the unexpected.

Growth Reflection

In the Past: Is there someone in your life who you loved in a way that shaped the outcome of your experiences with other people? How did the care for that person influence your perspective? What did it teach you about yourself?

In the Present: How do you approach the unexpected today? Do you feel able to handle difficult situations? How can you be even better equipped?

Thoughts

CHAPTER 7

AMBITION

Ambition: A strong desire to do or achieve something, typically requiring determination and hard work.

I AM NOT QUITE SURE how ambition came to be a bad word for a woman. Somehow that was the message I received growing up. An ambitious woman embodied self-centeredness, selfishness, self-interests, and self-absorption. (Did I miss any other self-focused words that begin with "self-"?) That "ambitious" label communicated a lack of the family values expected of a woman. Back then, in my mind, the only thing worse than calling a woman ambitious was calling her the B-word.

The summer before my first year of college, I attended a university transition program. I was a bright-eyed seventeen-year-old ready to take on the world. There were roughly twenty students in the program, with a handful of counselors and even fewer administrators. Young adults who were new to college life were given an opportunity to adjust to campus before the fall influx of students. A full summer of learning and adapting culminated in a celebratory banquet in a room filled with family and friends.

It was a delightful gathering, and the event climaxed when two counselors announced that awards were to be given to outstanding students. Most of the students perked up, including me, as the counselors stood at the podium. Every student in that room was a go-getter willing to give up their summer and start college early.

Without mentioning winners' names, the counselors created suspense by describing how each of the recipients embodied the qualities that earned them the award. This left everyone in the room wondering who would be called front and center to receive the prize. After sufficiently piquing the crowd's curiosity, they announced, "The award for most (insert your favorite superlative) goes to . . . !" The audience erupted into cheers and clapping to celebrate the owner of the accolade.

With each description of attributes, I would tell myself, *That's not me*. There was one description where I thought, *Hmmm, that could be me*, but it wasn't. I couldn't tell you how many awards were given out that day, but it wasn't many. The counselors were down to the last award. I'd sat in my fair share of award ceremonies at this point in my life, and I couldn't recall not being recognized in any of them. I was sure this day was going to break the streak. They began describing the recipient of the final award. I sat back in my chair and relaxed. Clearly it was not me. Then the counselor said something about persevering and gave a very specific example. I thought, *Wait, that is me.*

Then he said, "The award for 'most ambitious' goes to—Tori. . . ."

I relaxed in my chair again. *Nope, that's not me. Wait, did he just say my name?* I was glued to the chair. I hesitated. I heard my name, but it didn't seem right. I told myself, *He did not say my name.*

He was already looking at me, but he strengthened his gaze to sternly communicate that I needed to get up. I walked to the front with what must have been a confused look on my face. The reality is I was thankful to be recognized but I did not understand why they thought I was ambitious. I was debating with myself as I walked to the podium. *Calling me ambitious is not a good thing, but they're giving me an award for it, so it must be a good thing. I don't want to be the ambitious girl in the room. What will people think if I'm ambitious? I'm not ambitious.* I smiled and reluctantly accepted the award.

I approached the counselor after the ceremony and asked him why they thought I was ambitious. The look of confusion that found a home on my face earlier was now resting on his. He proceeded to give examples of how he and the other counselors observed me being proactive, persevering, and being a go-getter. I was still confused. I told him I did not think I was ambitious. He disagreed.

That young man must have thought I was ungrateful and maybe a little crazy. He probably wondered, *How could she be so smart and so ignorant?* I was more ill-informed than ignorant. I did not realize that the negative messages I'd received as a girl actually defined ambition incorrectly. My definition of ambition for a woman was one who is arrogant, selfish, and lacking the nurturing qualities that were expected of a woman, whereas my definition of ambition for a man was one who is proactive, perseveres, and is a go-getter. It was acceptable for a man to be ambitious, but an ambitious woman . . . blasphemous!

I did not realize that I had two very different definitions for the same word—the same word! This is why I was completely confused when they rewarded me for being ambitious. Like I said, the only thing worse than being ambitious was calling a woman the B-word.

I have always had a strong desire to succeed, but I still felt uncomfortable being labeled ambitious until the definition was presented in a way that helped me connect the dots. Several years after I was rewarded for being ambitious, I had the pleasure of meeting with a female executive at a Fortune 50 company. She shared with me that someone once told her that she was ambitious. Her recount of the story gave me the impression that it was not meant to be a compliment. Her response was brilliant. She said, "If by ambitious you mean . . ." and she proceeded to define what the word meant to her and how it applied to her role and commitment to excellence. She used descriptors that defined the mindset of a self-driven businesswoman and clearly aligned with serving others as a leader. Her definition was in sync with the *actual* meaning, but she took it further and made it her own.

It was a mic-drop moment. She succeeded at chipping away the last piece of unrefined, archaic marble from my brain. It was like a sculptor finishing a work of art, and the final tap of the chisel revealed a renewed mind. In one fell swoop she redefined ambitious, and I was 100 percent on board.

Definition and Perception

Words are powerful; they shape minds. My perception of the word "ambitious" did not change the definition. I once thought that the meaning of words changed based on value systems and culture. It is more accurate to say that meanings expand.

My first understanding of the word "dope" was illegal drugs. Then a dope was a person who lacked intelligence, and it also meant something was very good—as in "that's dope." If something was dope, it was cool. The cool meaning faded and made a comeback. Who knows if the word "dope" will even be relevant by the time you read this book. The word "bad" can mean good, "smoke" is no longer about barbecues, and "flossing" has gone way beyond teeth. The original definitions of the words still exist, but now they have new meanings in different contexts.

Culture impacts the meaning of words. Visit another country that speaks your native language, and you will quickly learn this is true. Words can even have different meanings regionally within the same country. Why is there so much variation? New meanings are evidence of experiences that alter our beliefs, impact our perceptions, and influence our culture. I experienced this when my perception of the word "ambitious" changed. My personal understanding did not change the original definition, but somehow culturally it expanded to have one application for a woman and another for a man. My dual interpretation did not change the original meaning, of course. The definition was the same.

Beliefs are the foundation for every culture—the culture in your home, your workplace, your community, and your country. Our beliefs inform our understanding, our understanding informs our perception, and if the belief is misaligned, then so is everything that follows. There may be people who believe that ambitious women are selfish. Some people think stay-at-home dads are not real men. Both opinions are rooted in a belief system that views the successful woman and the stay-at-home dad negatively.

You may recall studying theorems in high school. I appreciated theorems because while the general proposition may not be immediately evident as true, the chain of reasoning established by accepted truths establishes the proposition's truth. The key here is accepted truths, and if you don't believe accepted truths are the key, research the history of laws and how they have changed with culture. What was completely acceptable and legal in one generation is repulsive and illegal in another.

What was completely acceptable and legal in one generation is repulsive and illegal in another.

Learning What I Could Manage

Lukewarm Is Not Always Bad

When it comes to making decisions in life, being hot or cold—rather than lukewarm and uncertain—is lauded. Decisiveness is especially important in business, and full commitment is essential to success. Even with a firm and fully committed decision, some people need a warm-up or a break-in period. I remember leaving home for college excited about everything that lay ahead. Shortly after arriving, I missed my family and all the comforts of home. I was homesick. It was short-lived, however, and like most college kids I was able to work through my emotions quickly. In fact, I avoided calling my mom because I did not want her to rescue me. The summer program granted a lukewarm transition before the heat turned up at the start of the semester. It gave me time to adjust.

My experience that summer taught me something about change management. A stark change in environment or expectations can be daunting, and it can certainly evoke an emotional response in the person experiencing the change. Intuitively we know this, but we may not be as attentive or empathetic to how others process a change if we are not struggling ourselves. It's especially important to be mindful of this if we are responsible for leading people who may be undergoing change.

I loved playing outside when I was a kid, and cold winter days meant icy hands, even with gloves. I soaked up every ounce of fun until just before dinner, which meant I barely had enough time to get inside and wash my hands before parking at the table. I learned quickly that hot water on icy hands was painful, but lukewarm water was just right. This is true for our brains, too. Imagine implementing changes as an on-ramp to the highway and picking up speed. There will be times when the ramp is short or almost nonexistent and you simply have to hit the pedal and go, but often we can be intentional about the transition and allow the commitment and emotions to align.

Learning What I Could Influence

Rewards Are Inevitable

I would have been rewarded that summer even if I had not been recognized for being ambitious. I was thankful to be in a new environment with zero expectations about how I should perform or who I should be. Personal growth was my reward. While I was intrinsically motivated to do well and make the most of the experience, one of the best things about the summer program is that I did not expect to be rewarded. I was not competing for the highest grade-point average or the best project. The awards handed out that day were a surprise. Being rewarded for ambition was even more surprising. It was also without pretense. In my mind, I was simply learning, adapting to a different environment, and making new friends—nothing to reward. Little did I know there were observers taking notes.

There is always the option to come away from an experience better than you were before you had it and enjoy personal gratification, which is its own reward. But often someone is watching, and the recognition of others can manifest in positive ways. Your character and the quality of your work will position you to be rewarded, so never miss an opportunity to do good, even when no one is watching. A reward at its core is a consequence, an outcome, so to speak. Even weak or questionable character and poor-quality work are "rewarded." The reward may be in the form of fruitless relationships, a stagnant career, or termination from a role. Either way, rewards are inevitable.

Learning What I Could Control

The Choice Is Yours

Sometimes people see things in us that we don't see in ourselves. I have met many talented and capable people who did not recognize their own potential. I never grow tired of seeing the look of surprise on someone's face when I tell them that I believe they can do, be, or accomplish more than they are. Someone did the same for me by either assigning a task because they believed I could handle it or declaring they saw me at a level of success that I had not yet attained. We all need someone in our life who believes in us and believes more for us.

We all need someone in our life who believes in us and believes more for us.

Unfortunately, this goes both ways. People can also lead us to believe things about ourselves that are not true. Call someone stupid, lazy, or any other undesirable attribute during an impressionable stage of life, and they may have to work years to overcome the story they tell themselves or how others label them. If there aren't enough positive messages to offset the negativity, the building blocks of the mind create layers of poor self-image reaffirmed by negative self-talk that hinders growth. The final decision on who we want to be is ours to make, and that decision is made one choice at a time.

Success and failure are more predictable than many people realize. Simply weigh the outcomes of decisions and move accordingly. Life has taught me that too often we make decisions without considering the consequences (good or bad) and then deal with the aftermath. Even now, I can do a better job of sitting still and walking through the impacts of a decision before making it. The times that I have done this served me well. I recommend having quiet time alone to be thoughtful and/or prayerful before you add the perspective of a friend, family member, or mentor. No matter what advice or suggestions you receive, you get to live with your decision because no one else can own your choices for you.

Affirmation from others is helpful, but if you do not believe in yourself, all the encouragement and support in the world will not move you to your goal. No matter what anyone has ever said about you or will ever say about you, you get to decide if you are smart, proactive, resourceful . . . or ambitious.

Growth Reflection

In the Past: Have you learned that you had a limiting belief? What was your response when you became aware of it?

In the Present: List three to five qualities about yourself that you either identify with or have been labeled. Assess why they may or may not be accurate. Do these qualities support who you want to be?

Thoughts

CHAPTER 8

COLOR

Color: Pigmentation of the skin,
especially as an indication of someone's ethnicity.

I DO NOT IDENTIFY AS A WOMAN OF COLOR. I never felt a connection to the phrase "person of color," but I accepted it because it was common vernacular. That was until one day while speaking to an accomplished woman with an East Asian mother and a father of European descent who referred to herself as a woman of color, I realized that "of color" equals non-white in the United States. (In the US, her father would have been identified as white or Caucasian, and her mother would have been identified as Asian.) For years, I cringed when a black person referred to themself as a person of color, but I understood it. The reference to black Americans has ranged from colored to people of color. As I spoke to this woman, who did not identify as black, I realized "person of color" simply meant not white.

Isn't white a color?

If we identify everyone who is not white as a person of color, what we are really saying is white and other. White is a color, and so are brown, black, yellow, and red—all colors used at some point to describe the beautiful hues of people. When we say other, what we are really saying is there is a standard and the others are not the standard. Until we are all people of color, I'm not.

It's not unusual for kids to have a lot of pictures from childhood. School photos, family photos, candid photos—I have all of the above plus modeling photos. I started modeling as a toddler. As the story goes, my mother and I visited McDonald's for lunch and an agent sitting at a nearby table approached with the intent of finding her next child model. The Happy Meal was a big deal back then, and I don't know if the agent was staking out the local Mickey D's as a recruiting location, but it would have been a brilliant way to prescreen hundreds of kids a week. For the next few years, I traveled to photo shoots that would later appear in print ads and on toy boxes. I even appeared in a couple of episodes of *Sesame Street*. (Watching at home wasn't the same after experiencing my beloved characters flat and lifeless when the director yelled "cut.") Overall, it was a great experience. It felt like I was playing dress-up, meeting a lot of cool people, and experiencing a world much different than my life at home. I still have many of the ads I appeared in.

A few photo shoots stand out in my memory more than others. One of the unforgettable ones was for a children's clothing brand. The session took more time than most photo shoots due to the intricate set and wardrobe changes. Long shoots meant food breaks. During a break, I grabbed a snack and wandered around checking out the set. I landed near a board that had plans for the day and a description of the models. The note read "blonde, brunette, and other." I knew I wasn't the blonde. There was another little girl who was clearly the brunette. I quickly realized that I was the other. Talk about putting a damper on the day. I had to work harder to muster my happy face after seeing that. Several years after I stopped modeling, I sat down to reminisce by flipping through the plastic-lined pages of my portfolio. I realized that I was the only brown child in every photo. Some would say I should have felt special . . . exceptional, even, but I did not.

I was in high school the next time the exception status resurfaced. I had good relationships with several of my classmates. One was with a young man whose path crossed mine frequently because he and I were among the highest-performing students in our class. He told me his parents said he could not date a black girl, but I was an acceptable deviation. It was a *huh* moment—I had to shake my head to make sure I had heard him correctly. I'm sure he thought it was a compliment, but I did not. The exception status emphasized the "other" status.

Later in life, I was contemplating a career change, so I reached out to a man who was doing what I was considering so I could learn more. We met for lunch; he graciously answered all my questions and even asked a few thought-provoking ones to gauge my commitment level. I thought the meeting went well, and I gather he did also because he felt comfortable enough to ask if I planned to straighten my hair. I felt my head tilt and my eyes narrow (this was a combination of my confused and did-I-hear-you-correctly faces). I understood the question, but the bewilderment was genuine. There are a few ways to ask a question—one is with genuine curiosity, and another is to make a suggestion by presenting it as a question to appear less offensive. In this case, he was doing the latter—making a suggestion. I knew what he was asking, but I wasn't sure why a black American man would suggest . . . I mean ask . . . if I was going to straighten my hair. My guess was that he did not want my hair to offend others or limit my opportunities, but I preferred not to fill in the blanks, so I played along.

I asked, "Why would I need to straighten my hair?"

He responded that I didn't have "corporate hair."

"What is corporate hair?" I asked.

He paused and slowly responded, "You know."

Of course I knew, but it wasn't my idea, so I did not feel the need to clarify. He never ventured past the innuendo, but he had already defined it—corporate hair was straight hair. In his eyes, my hair was "other" hair, and it did not meet the standard.

A few years before this encounter, I had another interesting moment. My husband served in the United States military, and we lived in a quaint duplex on the military base. I appreciated that our neighbors were all skin shades and from every part of the nation. We took a liking to the newly married young couple who moved in next door. They took a liking to us as well. We were those borrow-a-cup-of-sugar type of neighbors. We broke bread together, spent time in each other's homes, and swapped recipes. They were from a Midwestern state established well after the Mason-Dixon line was drawn, and they had never seen the ocean. One of the first items on their to-do list was to drive to the beach. I had seen the ocean so many times that I never considered it could be a novelty for some people. I guess it would be like seeing snow for the first time as an adult—majestic.

One day the neighborly wife knocked on the door when she knew I was home alone. I was happy to see her as always. I invited her in, and as she sat down, it was obvious that this was not a borrow-a-cup-of-sugar visit. She sat on the sofa, and although she had sat there before, she seemed uncomfortable. She positioned her body on the front of the cushion with her knees close together and her back slightly rounded, and I was not sure why. The large window behind her bathed her back with sunlight, but I'd sat there hundreds of times, so I knew it wasn't heat that pushed her to the edge of the seat. After a few minutes of pleasantries, she asked, "Does it rub off?" I did not know what she was referring to, so I asked, "Does what rub off?" The question did not relate to anything she and I were discussing. It was as if she had been holding on to the question for too long, and it had suddenly spilled out. She rubbed her arm and then asked if my color rubbed off. I responded, "If it rubbed off, how would I shower?"

That moment was so impactful that I can still see her sitting on the couch. I can remember the dress I was wearing and how bright the sun was that day. It was a beautiful day. Understand, I did not intend to make her feel bad or appear condescending. The shower question was the first thing that came to my mind. Then I followed the shower response with, "I would have to reapply my color every day."

Her face showed what her brain was thinking. She hadn't reasoned through the sensibility of the question. I learned that day that until she met our family, she had only seen a black person on television. In her world, white was the standard, and the color for black people was added. I wondered what store sold black.

Everyone Is Ignorant

The word "ignorant" carries a negative connotation, but it simply means lacking knowledge, information, or awareness about a particular thing. Since none of us can know everything, we are all ignorant about something. Actually, we should be. Imagine the time it would take to know everything about everything. There is not enough time in one life to acquire that much knowledge.

Utilized knowledge is powerful. Education is required to acquire knowledge. Formal education is not necessary to erase ignorance, but formal or not, the transformation happens in the transition from not knowing to awareness and knowing and then to doing. It is the journey from uninformed drifting to deliberate execution, and execution requires action. People understand actions. While intentions may be good, they are not visible, and the only way to accurately convey intent is through aligned behaviors.

Have you ever said or done something that was socially unacceptable, but you were not aware of it until someone brought it to your attention? I certainly have, and it was due to my ignorance. I did not intend to offend; I lacked understanding. It is like walking into a home (or office) with outdated furniture and decor. There was a time when it was fashionable, and although those days are gone, the owner is oblivious. To them it's just home.

. . . the only way to accurately convey intent is through aligned behaviors.

We should all say a big thank-you to the people in our lives who are willing to make us aware of our "outdated furniture." They are like that acquaintance who is willing to tell you there is spinach in your teeth. If telling someone they have spinach in their teeth is uncomfortable, imagine the courage it takes to tell someone that what they said was offensive.

What would this world look like if we stayed curious about topics we don't fully understand? What if we made space to learn without making assumptions about other people or situations? Curiosity to quench ignorance is granted much more grace than uninformed certainty. The inquisitive person who seeks to learn about others, even when it's uncomfortable, is indicative of an open heart and mind. The person who is convinced they know it all already has a full cup.

A Little Black Is All Black

Growing up in a melting pot was great because I got to see all shades of people. Unlike my neighbor who had only seen black people on television, I saw black people every day. I also saw brown, tan, and all the various hues on the spectrum. One of my favorite rainy-day pastimes as a child was bringing images to life in a coloring book. I enjoyed it even more when the box of crayons was brand-new. The tips were sharp and fresh, but there were limited options for shading in skin tones. When I got to a character who would have been white, I picked a tan crayon. I wondered why we call people white if their skin is tan? Why do we call people black if their skin is brown? My child brain tried to understand the difference between skin color and race, and that box of crayons taught me that it was not logical.

Although some of the shades of skin were similar in my community, the accents and native languages revealed variety. I could walk into four stores on one street and hear a different language in each. I did not understand the languages, but I learned quickly that even people with similar skin tones could have different ethnicities. This was all clear to me, but there was one thing I did not fully grasp. There were kids in my neighborhood who had long wavy hair and bronze skin, and they were black. Another family with a silky chestnut-haired matriarch and a brood of beautiful daughters, all of them with buttermilk complexions and long dark silky hair, were black. Then there was the creamy-color man with the brushed-back billowing waves who lived on the corner. He was black too. The dark-chocolate girl with tight coils pulled into gravity-defying ponytail puffs and the blanched-almond boy with wispy curls that lay gently around his ears were both black. I wasn't sure how black was defined, but I quickly learned that a little black meant all black (which usually meant at least one black parent or grandparent).

My childhood curiosity wondered why a little white did not mean all white or why a little brown did not equate to all brown. There was something about adding black that nullified whatever else made the equation whole. The reality is we are all a hue on the brown spectrum, not much unlike dirt. From white kaolin clay to vibrant red loam and rich black soil, dirt, like people, comes in many colors. How humbling.

Learning What I Could Control

You Must Know Who You Are

I met someone who did not like chocolate. I didn't know that was possible. (I guess we learn something new every day.) I get chocolate not being a favorite, but completely disliking it was new to me. I'm sure he is not the only person on earth who does not like chocolate, but whether it's not liking chocolate, having curly hair, or your skin tone, you are who you are.

I learned at a young age that people have opinions. I learned at an older age that we cannot please everyone. It took me too long to stop trying, but knowing this should give all of us a measure of peace. Some people will think you should be thinner, be taller, have straighter hair, be more outgoing, or any other preference they deem a more desirable quality. You must know who you are. If you try to change your exterior or your interior to satisfy other people's perspectives of you, you will wake up one day and wonder who is looking back at you in the mirror.

I am a proponent of growth and becoming the best version of yourself. We have the power to identify and stop the behaviors that do not contribute to who we want to be. If there is something we want to start doing or get better at, we can choose to be proactive and create a plan to move us in that direction. Indecisiveness is almost as bad as doing nothing, except it grants us the gift of stress as we waver in our decision.

What do you like to do? What are you naturally good at? Recognize that these things may change as you do. Age, life stages, and personal growth tend to reveal new layers of our being that look slightly different than the previous model. Give yourself permission to be authentically you and evolve to an upgraded version.

Indecisiveness is almost as bad as doing nothing, except it grants us the gift of stress as we waver in our decision.

Learning What I Could Influence

Relationships Build Bridges

Being asked if my color rubbed off or if I planned to straighten my hair were awkward questions in the moment, but the connection between us made the person asking comfortable enough to ask. It is important to build relationships with people who don't look like us, think like us, or have the same background. This is how we build bridges and foster understanding. It is also how we dispel stereotypes and quench ignorance. I am happy to share that my cup-of-sugar friendship with my neighbor continued after that day.

It is easier to stay in our comfort zones by connecting with people who don't challenge, question, misunderstand, or disagree with our beliefs, but this creates silos and makes it almost impossible to build bridges. Many of us have mirror friends—when we look at them, we basically see ourselves. They look like us, think like us, and talk like us. It is natural to gravitate toward people we share interests and life experiences with, but the nature of growth requires us to have new experiences and stretch beyond our current space. Like I mentioned earlier, growth does not happen in the comfort zone. This is true for people interactions as well.

Learning What I Could Manage

Offenses Will Come

It is not a matter of *if* you will be offended but *when*. Offenses are inevitable, and sometimes they are accidental. The good news is that you can choose whether to feel offended or not. This may sound absurd, but it's true. Have you ever been cut off in traffic? How did you respond when that driver offended you? Did you lay on the horn, yell expletives, flip the bird, or maybe just fume in your car for several minutes thinking about how much of an idiot the other driver was? Perhaps you simply used your brakes so you didn't hit their car and kept driving like nothing happened.

There is something powerful about not allowing someone else's behavior to impact our day. Too often that offense stays with us and then we carry it to work and have a bad day. Then we take it home to affect the people we love. I doubt we want to give that brief moment and that driver that much power. Remember my lesson from chapter one: Be a duck.

Confidence Is Earned

I met with a woman who wanted to learn more about following my career path, and shortly into the conversation we began discussing the areas where she desired to grow. This led to anecdotes about personal and professional growth and development. I told her that there was a time when I cried easily and hated the thought of a difficult conversation. She could not believe it. I had to convince her that it took years to see the version of Tori that was sitting in front of her that day. Confidence is earned by overcoming challenges and trying new things that help you discover what you are capable of. It took overcoming challenges, getting knocked down, getting back up, and having uncomfortable conversations to build my confidence.

I had an aha moment one day while flipping through the channels and landing on a mixed martial arts match. The fighters were pounding each other, and neither contender showed any sign of giving in. I was especially fascinated by how one contender took repeated punches to the face. I couldn't help but think that if a professional fighter landed a right hook to my jaw, I'd likely fold, and the fight would be over—no thank you. Then I realized, the only way to get used to getting punched in the face is to get punched in the face. Most of us will never step in a ring to test our ability to handle jabs to the nose and body blows, but we will have opportunities to build our ability to take figurative punches.

If you don't have the resilience to endure hardship, challenges, criticism, or other ways to, as they say, earn your stripes, then prepare to live a mediocre life. Most worthwhile opportunities do not arrive uncontested.

Expect challenges along the way. When you know who you are (and depending upon your belief, *whose* you are), you can confidently persist through obstacles and disappointments.

Most worthwhile opportunities do not arrive uncontested.

I have also found that people who lack self-confidence tend to disappoint themselves. It is important to keep our word to others; it is also important to keep our word to ourselves. If you tell yourself that you are going to get up in the morning and work out, it is not a good idea to watch TV or scroll through social media until midnight. If you say you will avoid unhealthy foods to lose excess weight, don't purchase the sugar-laden snacks. If you've made a commitment to be an engaged parent or spouse, then be proactive about spending time with your family.

Making sacrifices is a part of achieving goals. Keeping our promises to ourselves aligns our words with our actions, and no one can show up for you better than you. When you keep your word to yourself, you build confidence in you. When you have confidence in you, others will too.

Growth Reflection

In the Past: Have you ever been offended by another person's perspective? Was there an opportunity to understand their reasoning and build a bridge?

In the Present: Do you have relationships with people who look, think, or believe differently than you? Is there an opportunity to enrich your understanding of the world with new relationships?

Thoughts

CHAPTER 9

NARRATIVE

Narrative: A way of presenting or understanding a situation or series of events that reflects and promotes a particular point of view or set of values.[9]

SOMETIMES YOU CAN SHAPE THE NARRATIVE EARLY, and sometimes you must employ damage control. I got to learn all about the damage-control part in the sixth grade, thanks to a childhood crush that created one of my least favorite things on earth—drama. A kind and quirky boy in my class (think '90s sitcom character Urkel without the glasses or the iconic voice) declared his love for me when we were only eleven. He was a

---

9 *Merriam-Webster Dictionary*, s.v. "narrative," accessed July 29, 2025, https://www.merriam-webster.com/dictionary/narrative.

nice kid, but I wasn't interested. There was, however, a girl who was very interested in him, but he refused to reciprocate her affection. She tried everything to get close to him. She sat near him at lunch, positioned herself in his line of sight at recess, smiled sweetly, and giggled with her friends when he passed in the hallway. I sat on the far end of the lunch table to put distance between me and him, and I still noticed her overt gestures. It was clear to anyone with one working eye that she would do anything within her power to get his attention, but he refused to take the bait.

One day she worked up the courage to tell him that she liked him and wanted him to be her boyfriend. He told her no and said, "I don't like you; I like Tori." The moment my name crossed his lips, in her eyes I became public enemy number one. That very same day she wrote me a note to inform me that I would soon be served a butt-whooping for stealing her man.

I was dumbfounded when I received the letter, but I knew exactly which "man" to talk to after I read it. I approached him and asked him what the fuss was about. He proudly recounted their conversation and how he gave her a firm no, told her he did not like her, and said his affection was set on me. He wanted to make sure she knew that she did not have a chance and that his stance was clear. I positioned myself squarely in front of him, closer than I ever had, and said his name matter-of-factly to make sure he gave me his full attention.

"You do realize that I do not like you," I reminded him. He was fine as a person, but I had zero romantic interest. He assured me that he was aware. So I asked, "Why did you even say my name? Why not just make it clear that you don't like her?" He looked a little puzzled and then asked why wouldn't he tell her that he liked me? I reminded him why he and I were talking in the first place, "Because now she wants to fight me because she thinks I stole you from her."

His face softened as he smiled, and his dreamlike gaze was evidence of why. The thought of me stealing him from another girl must have been almost as nice as me actually matching his affection. I said his name again to snap him back to reality. "You need to fix this. Go tell her that I do not like you, and I did not steal you from anyone." He snapped out of his dreamy state and said, "Okay, I'll tell her."

He did as promised, but she did not believe him. She thought it was a ploy to throw her off the scent. If looks could kill, she would have taken me out every time she saw me at lunch, at recess, or in the hallway. She made it clear that she had it in for me, and the friends she giggled with when her now ex-crush passed by followed her lead and gave me their ready-to-fight faces too. I just kept thinking how ridiculous it all was because I was already doing my best to stay away from lover boy so he wouldn't get the wrong message, and now I had to steer clear of her and her cronies too. This went on for weeks.

It all came to a head one day when I asked the teacher if I could take a restroom break during class. The halls were clear and quiet, with no students, teachers, or administrators in sight. I entered the bathroom expecting it to be empty, but to my surprise my nemesis and her sidekick were there drying their hands. They stopped and looked at me, and I did the same.

She had been threatening to beat me up, told her friends she was going to beat me up, and here I stood in front of her with no plans to get beat up. I knew the next few seconds were going to matter. I wasn't angry, just annoyed, and although I had no intention of being served a butt-whooping as she had promised, I had not come to the bathroom to fight. I had bio business to handle, so that's what I did. I walked past her and her friend and went into the stall, and when I came out, they were gone.

Miraculously, that day ended all the tension. She had her chance (and even had help if she wanted) to serve me the punishment she had been waiting weeks to deliver, and she did not take it. Something changed after that day. She couldn't look me in the eye anymore; she looked wounded. So one day I shocked her by sitting beside her so we could talk. I didn't want her to feel like I was her enemy because I wasn't, and there was no reason she and I could not be cordial to one another. We struck up a short-lived friendship, and she believed me when I told her that I never had a crush on her reluctant sweetheart. She confided in me that although she was treating him harshly, she still liked him and hoped he would be her boyfriend. She had been so upset that she could not think clearly, and the story that took shape in her mind did not align with anything she had observed in real life.

There were several opportunities for her to paint a more accurate picture of reality, but she held on to the part she wanted to believe. Eventually our friendship faded and so did her crush, but I learned a valuable lesson on narratives—sometimes you get to shape them, and sometimes you get to reshape them. They're going to take shape one way or the other.

Reshaping the narrative on the childhood crush conundrum was uncomfortable, but it was not hard. There were a few external factors to navigate and a misunderstanding to clear up, but none of it was dire. I was not fully aware of it at the time, but I had an internal narrative forming as well. It was influenced by images I saw on television, visits to the homes of friends with dads, and cultural depictions of families. I became keenly aware of how my story was different than what I was observing. I did not have the maturity to recognize how my self-image was being shaped or the wherewithal to form it differently.

One of my favorite narratives belongs to someone whose life was very different than my own. Few people get to live the storybook life of a young man named Solomon who was destined to become king. Solomon is regarded as the wisest and richest man to walk the earth. Depending on the resource, his wealth is estimated in the hundreds of billions (when adjusted for inflation). Some estimate his net worth in the trillions. Either way, Solomon's name is synonymous with wealth and wisdom. It is a part of his narrative. Those who know a little more about Solomon may mention that he had a thousand wives. (It was technically seven hundred wives and three hundred concubines, but who's counting?[10])

10 2 Samuel 11–12, 1 Kings 1–11.

What I find most interesting is that when the story of Solomon is told and retold, there is little mention of his flawed family. I've never heard anyone say, "Do you know that guy, Solomon? His parents committed adultery, and his father orchestrated the death of his mother's first husband after learning he got her pregnant with Solomon's older brother, who later died because of his father's indiscretion. Oh, and by the way, he was really rich and super smart." If Solomon felt any shame as a result of his parents' actions, there is no mention of it, and Solomon's story is boiled down to the wisest and wealthiest man to have walked the earth.

There is no doubt that Solomon's royal upbringing influenced his narrative early, and there is no evidence that he was plagued by his family history. Solomon was a prince destined to lead a nation. I have always admired people who connect to a purpose early and make it the North Star of their life. They live with intention. I don't know if Solomon began molding the king narrative early, but if he did not, that would be the one item on the short list of things he and I had in common. Perhaps if I had connected to a purpose earlier in life, I would have lived more intentionally.

For me, shaping the narrative primarily meant living bravely in the areas where I shone. It also meant living quietly in areas that might foster judgment, because judgment meant facing the shame that bubbled quietly beneath the surface. Once shame made its appearance, embarrassment came along for the ride. Embarrassment triggered feelings of inferiority that caused me to live apologetically without even realizing it.

I could not control the circumstance of my birth any more than Solomon could, but when my dad did not attend school functions, I lived quietly. When financial struggles reminded me that my single-parent household had fewer resources, I lived quietly. If I had a question that could have benefited from a fatherly perspective, I lived quietly. I shrank and retreated inward to the false safety of silence. Former first lady Eleanor Roosevelt said, "No one can make you feel inferior without your consent." She's right, and I gave full consent for my narrative to make me feel inferior.

A visit with a friend taught me a simple but powerful lesson. The two of us sat in her living room for hours laughing and enjoying our time together when she realized there was something that she wanted me to see in her closet. We would have to walk through her bedroom to get there. As we approached the room, she asked me to excuse her mess. I assured her that I was not concerned with the state of her room; I only felt gratitude for the visit and our time together. As we entered the room, she began to point out the few things that she deemed imperfect and apologized for them. I reassured her that there was no need to point out the few items out of place. Her bed was made and overall the room was neat and tidy, but she kept drawing my attention to what she viewed as imperfections.

I don't remember what she and I talked about that day or what she showed me in her closet. The thing that stuck with me was that she was cognizant of something I would not have paid attention to and apologized to me when no offense or harm was committed. She made me wonder how often I was living apologetically for something that no one cared about and wasn't harmed by. Was there an area where I was being unnecessarily sensitive to judgment? I cared about my friend—her well-being, her success, and her family. I did not care about the few items out of place in her bedroom. If the perceived imperfections did not matter to me, how much more would they matter to someone who did not know her at all? Of course, she would not have welcomed them to see her closet, but you get my point.

Most of the time, the only person who concerned themselves with my insecurities was me. I have never lacked friends, and even the few moments of judgment that I endured were brief. (Negativity has an inherent stickiness to the psyche.) Of course, there may be an occasional someone who wants to write you off because there is something about you that they deem unsavory. My experience has been that most people like you for who you are, and if for some reason they don't like you, once they have an opportunity to get to know you, the slant is toward like. Folks care about how you treat them and others, whether you show up when it counts, and if they generally want to be around you.

The stories we tell ourselves about ourselves are deeply personal. They may swim in our minds for years, stringing a themed thread through relationships and experiences, convincing us to believe the best or worst about who we are while influencing the behaviors that reinforce them. How we see ourselves impacts how we believe others perceive us and how we see them. If you want to live a different story, then change the narrative.

The same way Solomon's story is shaped by wisdom and riches, our narratives are based on what is most prominent about us, and we get to choose what that will be by the choices we make and the consistency of our character.

We Only Know in Part

Narratives can be interesting because oftentimes we only see part of the story, usually the part we want to see or that is meant to be seen. This is why it is important to get to know and see people from different angles. It cultivates authenticity and builds closer relationships. Have you ever spent a significant amount of time with someone in a professional or academic setting and then after months, maybe years, of only seeing them in one light, you see them with their family?

I find it especially rewarding if young children are a part of the equation. I've experienced this a few times. It is refreshing to see people in comfortable settings with their loved ones. Children make it even more memorable. They say what they're thinking, express what they're feeling, and behave in whatever way their hearts desire. Toddlers do not care about narratives. They are as genuine as it gets. Spend five minutes with a talking tyke, and you'll know exactly what I mean.

I once worked with a man who intentionally disconnected himself from his colleagues. He could have fallen off the face of the planet, and maybe four people in the company would have noticed. He made it clear that he did not want to build relationships with anyone. I was shocked when I received a Christmas card from him. The card had photos of his family, and suddenly, I realized that there was a whole part of him that none of us knew. He looked happy. His card reminded me that we often only observe a partial picture, and seeing him in a different light affirmed that we were experiencing only a fraction of his story.

Learning What I Could Control

Persistence Does Not Always Pay Off

I have always admired persistence. It takes resolve to push forward, especially when the terrain is rough. The reward is that much sweeter when the outcome is as desired. Personally, it is hard for me to throw in the towel. It takes wisdom to know when to call it quits, but I have enough personal and professional examples to know that sunk costs are real. Wise persistence pays off, but remaining steadfast on a dead-end road or, even worse, a road that ends with a disastrous drop-off is not a good use of time, money, or energy. A person who cares about outcomes does not want to be known as a quitter, but those childhood crushes taught me a valuable lesson—persistence does not always pay off. We must know when to cut our losses. Lover boy's pursuit of me only pushed me further away. His crush's pursuit of him was fruitless. No one's persistence paid off. Sometimes we must walk away and shift our energy into more productive pursuits.

Quitting too soon can be just as damaging as pursuing too long. It is important to know when to call it quits. I must add a disclaimer here. There are a few things in life that I don't believe ever deserve quitting. One of those is family. Relationships can have interesting dynamics, and sometimes we must protect our mental or emotional well-being, but for the most part, familial bonds are special. And by family, I don't only mean those related by blood. There are some friends that love like family.

You should also never quit on you. Always believe in yourself. You are gifted, and even if you are not quite sure what your gifts are, trust me, you have them. Sometimes we are too busy to realize what makes us unique in this world, and tucking away quietly from the hustle and bustle of life (including television and social media) will allow you to connect with yourself. I am a fan of occasionally disrupting the normal routine for the sake of stimulating the mind in a new way. Most things on earth can be replaced, but you and the people you love are one of a kind.

Learning What I Could Influence

Inadvertently or Intentionally

I could be completely wrong, but I don't think most people live day to day thinking about the story of their life. Social media certainly creates space to convey the image we want others to see, but life keeps us busy, and unless there is a reason to intentionally shape a narrative, most of us don't.

You should know that your life will have a narrative whether you shape it or not. Our kids and loved ones will tell stories about us that convey who we are or who they perceive us to be. Some folks call this legacy. No one in my circle thought about or mentioned this as I was growing up, and for that reason, rarely did I see anyone living life intentionally. Life was more about surviving. Arguably, the impact most of us make will not be remembered beyond our families, but even in our immediate sphere of control, that impact cannot be minimized. It has the potential to reverberate through generations. We can choose to have a positive and meaningful influence.

Our narrative will be molded by our attitude and our most consistent behaviors. We can tell whatever story we want about ourselves; in reality, the story that will get told (and retold) is the story others believe to be true. Most people don't need an image consultant, but it would be helpful to think about who we want to be and how we impact others during our time on earth. Then comes the execution. What will it take to make that our story?

Our narrative will be molded by our attitude and our most consistent behaviors.

If you want to be a great spouse, then be intentional about the time spent together and how you treat your significant other. Maybe you want to be the best parent. This requires a lot of patience, planning, and sacrifice for your children and ultimately your family. Perhaps you want to make an impact on your community. Consider the people you need to connect with and how relationships multiply your efforts. Your desire could even be to make a difference in your workplace. Whatever your motivation, you have a part to play in the intentionality of the outcome.

Some people take life as it comes. We do the next thing that is expected of us or manage whatever lands on our plate. Some people strategically plan and prepare the next steps. Life is not coming at them. They are coming at life. I was 100 percent in the first camp. I never had a dream. My mantra was work hard, operate with excellence, be kind, and doors will open. They did, but I never planned in the direction of any particular door.

The author of *Alice's Adventures in Wonderland*, Lewis Carroll, captures this sentiment perfectly: "If you don't know where you are going, any road will get you there." I have been blessed with some amazing roads, but thankfully I learned to dream. Before I had a dream of my own, my goals were unintentionally tied to someone else's dream. For some, this looks like going to the college or pursuing the career path desired by parents. For others, it may mean helping someone grow their business when you are fully capable of building your own. It's not necessarily bad to have your dreams and goals tied to someone else's if you have an opportunity to fulfill your life's purpose and passions as well.

It is even better if your dream is intentionally connected to someone else's dream. The amplification through collaboration has the potential to benefit more people.

You Have Influence

We can only control the narrative to a degree. Controlling the narrative fully would be telling someone else how to think and what to feel. We can influence how people perceive us, but since everyone has free will, each person will experience you through their own filter.

Remember, the narrative will be shaped whether you influence it or not. The kid labeled goody-goody may appreciate rules and order, and the kid labeled wild may simply enjoy adventure and taking risks. This goes for adults, too. The narrative may even be impacted by the company we keep. Spend time with high-flyers and others will assume you are smart and successful. Hang with people who are not doing much with their life and you may be labeled a loser by association. My mother used to tell me that birds of a feather flock together. Along those same lines, the author and motivational speaker Jim Rohn is credited with saying you are the average of the five people you spend the most time with. Choose who influences you and who you influence wisely.

Learning What I Could Manage

Rejection

Rejection can cause embarrassment, and embarrassment does not feel good at any age. We may not embarrass as easily as we get older, but it is still an icky feeling. I do not know if others were present when my self-proclaimed nemesis confessed her affection for our classmate, but her crush's rejection crushed her. That would have stung for anyone who campaigned for weeks to get their sweetheart to notice them. An audience would have made his refusal worse. When he added, "I like Tori," he twisted the knife. I commend the girl's bravery in sharing how she felt, but his rejection fostered anger. All the energy she felt was shifted from the object of her affection to the object of her aggression.

We've already talked about how blinding emotions can be, and somehow at that young age I knew that she wasn't truly mad at me. I did not have the language for it back then, but I knew she was mad at what I represented—the pain of the rejection and the roadblock between her and her sweetheart. Perhaps I did not reciprocate her anger because deep down inside, I knew what rejection felt like for a different reason.

Rejection hurts, but it wasn't until I was an adult that I began to ask myself why rejection hurts. For me, the core of rejection meant I did not feel liked or loved. The more I learned to love myself, which came as a result of knowing who I am and my faith, rejection became easier. Being likable does not mean we will be liked by everyone, and that is okay. There will be times when we experience rejection for simply doing what is right. The good news is you will not lose any sleep over that one.

Authenticity Reveals Love

We can portray the narrative that we want others to see, or we can be our authentic selves and let the story play out as it will. Living with intention is great when people know the real you. Then they get to decide if they want to share their time, their space, and ultimately their life with you. The one thing we cannot get back is time, and when we share it with someone, we are choosing to give them a part of our existence. Our imperfections, when known, reveal who really loves us. This can be liberating.

The one thing we cannot get back is time, and when we share it with someone, we are choosing to give them a part of our existence.

People will either love the real you or an image of you. If you want authentic love, share the authentic you.

What If?

Have you ever played the what-if game? Oftentimes, it is played without the realization or intent to play it. You start by identifying something in your life that doesn't meet your standards of satisfaction. Then you wonder how your life would be different if you could change it. I used to ask, *What if I had grown up with both of my parents?* I imagined some of the ways I thought my life would have been different. I can't say that it would have been better or worse. I can say that I am thankful for every experience I've had because I learned from them.

I realized the crux of the what-if game is discontent. The moment I identified the thing I wanted to change, I was acknowledging that I did not see the good that came from it or appreciate the current circumstance. Today, with a grateful heart, I can say that I would not change anything. Every heartache and mistake led me to right now, and why on earth would I want to change that?!

Growth Reflection

In the Past: Is there an area of your life or a past experience where you wish you had made a different decision? Knowing that you cannot change the past, what can you learn from it?

In the Present: Is it important to you to build a legacy, even within your family? Are you intentionally making decisions to position those around you to be better as a result of you being your best?

Thoughts

CHAPTER 10

COMPARE

Compare: To examine the character or qualities of especially in order to discover resemblances or differences.[11]

WE LIVE IN A CULTURE OF COMPARISON. All through primary school, my classmates and I were lined up shortest to tallest. Most of the time I landed somewhere in the middle, but I felt accomplished if I ended up closer to the back of the line because taller was better. Science projects were compared, along with grades, and in physical education classes, value was placed on the fastest and the strongest. Almost everything was compared, even without being prompted by adults to do so. We placed our

---

11 *Merriam-Webster Dictionary*, s.v. "compare," accessed July 29, 2025, https://www.merriam-webster.com/dictionary/compare.

little growing palms against one another's to see who had the biggest hands, and we placed our shoes side by side to see whose foot was largest. Comparison was (and still is) the foundation for competition, and I have always enjoyed competing. When it was within my power to be the best, I wanted to be number one.

I can't pinpoint the moment when my best-at-everything desire started to fade, but there were moments in high school when the goal of chasing the top spot began to lose its luster. I still wanted to be great at the things I cared about, but not at everything.

One of those moments was in a high school chemistry class. I was eager to finally take the class, but I quickly realized that I did not like the subject. (Hats off to all the chemistry lovers out there.) My chemistry teacher was a polite and pragmatic woman, and although neither of us ever talked about her class not being my favorite, my lack of enthusiasm was evident. I am sure she was aware that I did not enjoy her class. I studied enough to do the work but not enough to be great at it. I did, however, put effort into studying for her final exam. I felt ready the day she placed the test on my desk. All the studying paid off until I came to one question that I knew the answer to but was unable to recall. It was like that word that sits on the tip of your tongue but refuses to come out. It was stuck in my brain, gnawing at me. I knew it was there, but I could not get it to manifest.

I sat in my seat thinking for what felt like a long time. I tend to look up when I'm pondering. If I'm really pensive, my head tilts to the side. This is what happened as I was fishing through the folds of my brain for that answer. As my head began to reset to neutral, my eyes landed on the paper of the student next to me. I could see her answer to the same question I was wrestling to recall. A fleeting sense of relief swept over me: *Aha, that's it!* It was immediately followed by *Ugh, you didn't recall it; you saw it.* I did not write the response on the paper. I left that question blank and got it wrong.

During the next class, the teacher called each student up one at a time to show us our grade on the final exam and what our overall grade would be in the class. I don't recall what my grade was on the exam, but all the other grades along with the final made my course grade a 92.4; a 93 was an A. I thought to myself, *So close to an A.* She put the grade book down, looked me straight in my eyes, and told me that she would have given me the one-tenth of a point that would have rounded my grade up to a 93, but she did not feel like I tried hard enough in her class, so I would have to settle for the B. I don't know if she expected me to plead my case. I did not tell her that I had studied for that exam or inform her that chemistry was not my best subject. I didn't even appeal for mercy. She was right. I did not try hard in her class. I studied enough to get by, and if that meant not cheating and taking a B, then so be it. I said, "Okay," and went back to my seat.

I was never satisfied with a B, but I was satisfied with the realization that I would not be great at everything. I also discovered that I did not want to be great at everything. Excelling at anything requires time and energy, and that day was the beginning of me learning that I did not want to use my time or energy in that way. There were some things that I did not care about, and I did not want to pretend that I did. It would be a few more years before I concluded that my worthiness was not based on a score or a metric, but I give credit to the chemistry class for planting a seed.

Not too long before that chemistry class, I wanted to be great at everything asked of me, especially when grades were involved. Report cards and end-of-grade test score comparisons were a big deal back when my age was a single digit. (They still are for many kids.) Nine-year-old me was shocked when a boy in my class told me that he was getting paid five dollars for every A on his report card. I thought, *Five dollars for every A! I can hit the jackpot every nine weeks.* Not only was his report card incentivized, but it was also monetized. (The value of that money has more than doubled in today's dollars, but my guess is many kids would still gladly take the five.) That evening, I told my mother about the boy at school who was getting paid for his grades and asked if I could have five dollars for every A on my report card. I knew that getting a yes was a longshot, but her response surprised me. She did not even crack a smile and said, "Why would I pay you for something you are supposed to do? And you're smart, so that's not hard for you anyway." (*Bum bum bum* . . . cue the game-show contestant loser music.) I was disappointed, but the lack of payment did not stop me from the pursuit to be the best.

I have competed a lot over the course of my time on earth.

As a child, the competition mostly centered on grades, sports, or clubs. I have also competed a fair amount as an adult, but there was one competition I would not have given a second thought to if it had not been for the encouragement, perhaps prodding, of a teacher. My years growing up were a delicate balance between rough-and-tumble and a classic display of my generation's definition of femininity. The wrestling coach approached me to join his team after I fouled out of a basketball game. Shortly after, a teacher tried to convince me that I should enter the high school beauty pageant. I told them both that I was not interested. However, the beauty pageant believer and I crossed paths daily, and she was persistent. I was adamant that pageants were not my thing, and she was adamant that I could take home the crown. She was persuasive and I admired her, so I agreed to participate.

My goal was to make the experience as painless as possible. I borrowed a dress from my cousin and took a detour to the local department store's makeup counter on my way to the pageant. (The beauty consultant was more than happy to spruce me up before the big event because my daily makeup routine consisted of applying lip balm.) There was no fanfare when I arrived at the school that evening. I parked in the same lot I parked in each morning, and I walked in the same door I used to enter the building each day. The hall was eerily quiet. I strolled down the dark, locker-lined corridor with the dress slung over my shoulder and wondered if I had possibly arrived on the wrong day. That was, until I opened the backstage door. The frenzy of makeup, hair, and wardrobe reminded me of behind the curtain at a fashion show. I felt out of place because clearly my expectations did not match the energy in the room.

In fact, I had zero expectations. I was there because a teacher did a great job convincing me, and my financial investment was minimal. All I had to do was slip into the dress I borrowed, make sure I remembered the words to my speech (if I made it far enough in the rounds to deliver it), and get through the evening. I was calm backstage as I watched several young ladies take deep breaths to work through their nerves. My lack of nervousness made me feel out of place, but the moment I entered stage left and saw the bright lights, flashing cameras, and audience, my heart began to race. I realized that I'd underestimated what I'd said yes to. I'd convinced myself that this was not my kind of scene. I would not even have been a spectator that evening, yet there I was on stage . . . competing.

I had been in the auditorium many times, but that evening was different. The school was older than most of the people in it, and the same wooden folding seats, with a spring tough enough to reclaim their retracted position if I lifted my legs only slightly off the ground, were not full of students. They were full of people of all ages supporting their favorite contestant on a glamorous evening as they patiently awaited the outcome. The dark, heavy curtain that masked backstage nuts and bolts had never looked so elegant, and the judges' station positioned front and center made everything feel official.

The anticipation and tension grew with each round. As the

contestant count narrowed, I watched young ladies who were normally cordial toward others shift to cold shoulders. Some were still kind, but a few made it clear that everyone else was in their way, and their body language said everything that their mouths did not. I couldn't have cared less about winning when I walked into that building with my borrowed dress and pit-stop makeup, but as the rounds progressed, so did my desire to compete. Once I made it to the round where contestants had to deliver their speech, it was game time. Although I was not a seasoned pageant contestant, I did compete in speaking events with the FFA. (Future Farmers of America will always have real estate in my heart.)

In fact, I wrote the pageant speech while traveling for an FFA competition. I was refined in the fiery crucible of public speaking, so when I approached the mic, everything about that moment was familiar, except for the skinny heels on my shoes. The peering eyes, the deafening silence of the crowd, the lights bearing down on my face, and the judges with pens in hand ready to assess my performance were comfortably uncomfortable. I steadied myself for the delivery as my mom watched from the crowd.

It was unusual for my mother to attend extracurricular activities. On another special but less glamorous night, a crowd gathered in the school gymnasium for senior lettering night. This was a much-anticipated high school event celebrating athletes. Our coach's wife, who was also one of my favorite teachers, escorted me to center court to receive my letter. I thought the world of her, so I was wholly appreciative and honored that she did that for me. The next day at school, multiple kids approached me to tell me that they did not know my mom was white. I giggled and said, "She's not." Then I asked them why they did not recognize the teacher, but the reality was they did not recognize my mom. I understood that my mother had to work a lot, so her being there the night of the pageant elevated the significance of the event.

As large as the auditorium was, that night at the pageant it felt small and intimate as I stood front and center to deliver the speech. The delivery felt smooth in the moment, and the look of pride on my supporters' faces was energizing. The only line I can remember is one that has been stated and restated so many times that it is hard to know who deserves credit for it. "God's gift to us is who we are. Our gift to God is who we become." Eleanor Powell and Hans Urs von Balthasar both have a version that occasionally surfaces to inspire the masses. It certainly inspired me, and I delivered that along with the rest of the speech before a rousing round of applause ushered me back to my mark near center stage.

As the evening advanced to the final round, all the young ladies contending for the crown stood side by side. The beautiful gowns, classy hairstyles, and skillfully applied makeup were a far cry from what we wore to school every day. The spotlights, flashbulbs, and cheering merged into a sea of sounds that made my beating heart feel fast and steady. Suddenly, I realized that I was tired of smiling. I had never held a smile that long. My face muscles began to fail just as I was saved by the announcer.

It was the moment everyone had been waiting for. Each finalist's name was called. The crowd cheered and the energy increased as the number of contestants on stage grew smaller. I was still in the running, and it was time to announce the winner. My heart abandoned its steady pace and began to race. The anticipation in the room was palpable. My mom was clearly in my line of sight, and she looked proud.

The emcee paused and then boldly announced, "The winner is . . ." The volume spiked as the sea of voices erupted into celebratory cheers, clapping, whistling, and shouting.

I won . . . I was declared the winner!

Within seconds a crown was placed on my head, a sash was draped over my gown, and a long red robe covered my shoulders. I had forgotten all about my zero expectations from earlier in the evening. Within a few hours, I went from reluctant to royalty . . . pageant royalty.

Not much changed in my world after winning that pageant. My pageant-believer teacher was beaming with pride, which made me feel accomplished, and the congratulations trickled in for a few days after, which I was grateful for, but overall, I felt like Tori. It was similar to the feeling of having a birthday. There is cake and ice cream and maybe even a party. You are a year older, but when you wake up the next day, you feel the same age you were the day before your birthday. At least that's how I feel when birthdays come around. There was, however, a small shift internally. I surprised myself because I did well at something that I would not have considered on my own, and it increased my confidence to try new things that I might not have an obvious affinity for.

Measurable outcomes are easy to compare. Whether it is grades, sports, or competing in a pageant, the result is easy for all to see and evaluate. I have competed in enough arenas to recognize when I was passionate about the result and when I was not. I walked into the chemistry class with the expectation to be great, only to realize I was not passionate enough to dedicate the energy it took for that outcome. I walked onto the pageant stage with no expectations and realized that I had what it took to be great on that day.

I have excelled at most things I put my mind to. I give my mom credit for teaching me and my sister to believe in ourselves early on. When we were kids, she would say, "If there is a will, there is a way" followed by "You can do anything you put your mind to." I believed her, and I believed I could accomplish anything I focused my effort on. The belief was so strong during my formative years that later in life I jokingly say it's a good thing that I did not believe I could fly because I might have jumped off the roof just to test it. I was not afraid to try, and I did not fear comparison or competition because I learned early that it is a part of the success landscape.

I don't agree with every aspect of the comparison game, but I understand its nature. Sometimes we are compared without realizing that it's even happening. Comparison and therefore competition are inevitable, but the good news is we get to choose the things we care enough about to compete for.

Learning What I Could Control

Integrity Is More Valuable than Winning

The saying "Cheaters never prosper" was popular when I was growing up. Integrity was important. There are a few timeless principles appreciated by the human race. Honesty, kindness, respect, and fairness are a few of them. When I couldn't remember the answer to the chemistry exam and then I saw it on my classmate's paper, I could not write it on my exam because it was not the right thing to do. I remember the result because of the consequences. The final grade was about more than that class. That B impacted my grade-point average, class ranking, and perhaps even scholarship opportunities. I acknowledged that I was never satisfied with a B, but I was not willing to do something I felt wasn't right to get an A.

When I was younger, I understood integrity to mean doing the right things outwardly. The day of the exam cemented my understanding of doing the right things inwardly. It was about being honest with myself. The root meaning of integrity is wholeness, or a state of being complete. I had to live in my skin beyond that day, and that would have been difficult if I had written that answer on my paper.

In the professional arena, I have had the pleasure of helping entrepreneurs with their businesses, and a few of them have struggled to get the results they planned for. It is better to honestly give 110 percent and fall short than to cut corners and make it. I remind them that numbers are a measure of effectiveness, not worthiness. Integrity beats winning any day of the week in my book. In fact, integrity *is* the win.

Jack of All Trades, Master of None

Trying to be great at everything will likely put you in the all-around-average category. Being great at anything requires a time investment, and when I was a kid, it seemed like a day was as long as the universe is wide. We had all the time in the world. I managed to get my homework done and still have time to play outside for hours, watch television, and read books. As I got older and had more obligations, there never seemed to be enough hours in the day. The realization of this started in high school with a part-time job, clubs, and sports added to my academic obligations. Suddenly, it became important for me to prioritize.

Think about anyone you know who is great at something. It could be playing a sport or an instrument. Many people have a natural inclination to excel at something, but even they must dedicate time to hone their skill. If we are gifted in multiple areas, we could be good at many things, but we won't be great at anything without focus and dedication. (I learned this in chemistry class.)

I believe everyone has a gift—something we are good at. That gift has the potential to be a superpower. We must spend time developing our strengths because someone in this world needs our gift. Not only will we be great at it, but our existence will be more enjoyable. You will feel like you are winning at life. If you want a worthwhile comparison, compare winning to losing. Winning is more fun.

Proof

It took many years for me to connect with and embrace purpose, but the fact that you are reading this book is evidence that I did. The glimmer was there early, but I ignored it. I loved books as a kid, and I don't just mean reading them. I enjoyed seeing them on shelves, feeling the spine in my hand, and flipping through the pages.

One of my favorite elementary school pastimes was sitting in my tiny bedroom closet while reading. The closet was small and dark, which meant I had to bend my knees to fit and use a flashlight to see, but I didn't mind; my little bent legs served as a perch for my book. I looked forward to the days the teacher took the class to the library, and I enjoyed visiting the public library when I was old enough to go on my own. I still get a warm feeling when I walk into a library or a bookstore. It feels like home. I thought most people shared my affinity for books. Didn't everyone read the inside page with the publisher information when they were a kid? I couldn't be the only kid who looked forward to cozying up with a blanket and a good book. Surely all kids read books until they fell asleep.

I remember reading a novel in the fifth grade and entertaining the thought that I should be a writer when I grew up.

The moment was brief, and I did not hold on to it. I loved when my sixth-grade teacher gave creative writing assignments, but I thought of it as schoolwork and not a passion. Writing felt like fun, not work, and work is what was required of adults. Every message I received as a child was to do well in school, go to college, and get a job, so I never revisited my childhood love. I've had other passions over the years and successfully fulfilled some professionally, but what you are holding in your hand is evidence of me not worrying about comparisons and instead pursuing my purpose.

Writing was not my only passion, but it is the one I ignored more than any other. Remember what I said a few chapters back about opportunities and timing? Apparently, I needed to live a little before I could fulfill this passion. This book is proof that it is never too late.

Learning What I Could Influence

Square Pegs and Round Holes

I have met people who have wasted a tremendous amount of energy agonizing about something they want to change about themselves that they have absolutely no control over. Everyone has natural strengths and abilities. Sadly, some of us never discover or use them because our attention was shifted in directions that don't maximize our God-given potential, or we spent too much time comparing ourselves with something or someone, which does not serve us well. This is one reason why it is important to have people in our lives who believe in us and give us honest feedback, similar to my pageant-believer teacher. She saw abilities that I could not see on my own. It is also helpful to have people in our lives who are willing to tell us hard things that we may not want to hear.

There was a period in my career when I was responsible for hiring. I quickly learned that it was not wise or fair to ask square pegs to fit in round holes. (A round peg may fit in a square hole, but do know that something is lacking.) It was not good for the business, and it was not good for the candidate. The sad part was that oftentimes, square pegs wanted to force themselves into round holes. Some people convince themselves that they will fit or they can make it work. We can only operate outside of our gifts for a short time. I believe there are a lot of miserable people surviving in jobs they hate because they either don't know their gifts or they're not utilizing them in their current role.

I once worked with a man who felt like he had to operate outside of his natural disposition to be successful in his role. He was naturally reserved and quite reticent in social settings, but he presented himself as gregarious. He compared himself to others and worked hard to become the person everyone wanted to do business with.

One day he came to my office door, and I almost did not recognize him. He looked the same, but he wasn't the same. He was slouching and disheveled, and the cadence of his speech was unfamiliar. The customary friendly smile was gone. He told me that he was tired, and he would not be around much longer. I asked why, because he seemed to be doing so well. The team enjoyed working with him and customers liked him. He confessed that he had been pretending to be kind, hospitable, and friendly, and although he was nice, he said he was not nearly as nice as he seemed. I suggested he try doing the job as himself. He paused and then said it wouldn't work. He left shortly thereafter. The round peg was exhausted from trying to fit in the square hole. His conclusion: He wasn't a good fit.

Pressure to Perform

Comparison increases the pressure to perform. Add a deadline, and the sense of urgency intensifies. That intensity creates pressure, and the pressure, either viewed as a privilege or a burden, has the ability to produce results.

I learned at a young age that there is a trio that can get most humans to do almost anything: money, position, and power. We should not be surprised by questionable behavior if any or all of these are at stake. In school it shows up in the form of scholarships, class rankings, and limited or exclusive opportunities regarded for a few. In the professional world it may manifest as a raise or bonus, a leaderboard, or a promotion. Competition can bring out the best in people. It can also bring out the worst.

The push to get results through comparisons motivates the competitive to compete harder, and unfortunately, it can also inspire foul play. Aside from the foul play, it is almost impossible to get full collaboration on a team that internally compares or ranks its members. There will undoubtedly be one or a few who prioritize themselves over the team and refrain from sharing without reservation to maintain a competitive edge and perceived positional superiority. Like the cold shoulders I experienced in the pageant, a lot can be hidden behind a smile.

As dire as that may sound, comparison and competition can be good. They inspire innovation and force us to improve our skills. Imagine going to a sporting event without a scoreboard. We would have no idea who was winning. The comparison keeps us engaged and focused. My advice: Play fair and you will have nothing to lose.

Learning What I Could Manage

Thief of Joy

Theodore Roosevelt said that comparison is the thief of joy. Do you know someone (or maybe you are that someone) who was content with their pay until they learned that a co-worker with a similar role earned more? Maybe you purchased that new shiny thing, and you were happy with it until someone showed up with a nicer and newer shiny thing. Suddenly, yours seemed less shiny. I was disappointed when I learned the boy in my class was being paid for his A's and I would not be paid for mine. As it turned out, my disappointment was short-lived, and

I was motivated to do well without the payment. But it is easy to forget our blessings and dwell on what we don't have.

Gratitude is the foundation of joy. Anytime we feel down because of what we lack, we can be thankful for all that we already possess and refuse to allow comparison to steal our joy. A grateful heart grants contentment even as we are striving to be our best.

Resistance Is Good

There was a time when I resisted resistance. Then I learned that resistance made me better. It all made sense when I learned about the Biosphere 2 experiment conducted in Arizona in the 1990s. It was a complex undertaking, but for simplicity, visualize a multi-acre greenhouse with electrical, plumbing, and mechanical systems supporting multiple biomes—a biological community—and the people who lived in it for the duration of the experiment.[12]

I was fascinated by what they learned about trees. The trees grew to a certain height within the enclosed space and then—what seemed like spontaneously—fell over. Picture it: A tree that looks perfectly healthy suddenly falls over with no clear explanation. What could be causing this? The environment lacked wind, so it wasn't a gust that blew them over. Ironically,

---

12 For information about Biosphere 2, see https://biosphere2.org/about/about-biosphere-2.

it was the lack of wind that caused the trees to collapse. They needed wind to build rigor and remain standing. Stress wood, as it is called, builds the resistance needed for a tree to stay upright.

This is not unique to a greenhouse environment. Even in a natural forest, the trees on the outer edges are better able to withstand wind simply because they encounter it more.[13] Trees need resistance to grow healthily. Imagine that. They essentially needed something pushing against them to reach their optimal state. They needed stress. Resistance is a blessing if we want to get better.

The resistance needed to achieve great things comes in many forms. Whatever you are up against has the power to strengthen you. The "winds" that build our resistance may look different than the winds others face. They may look different than what we expect. But you can learn to grow with the resistance.

Resistance is a blessing if we want to get better.

My journey is my journey. Your journey is your journey, and all comparisons are not bad (we do need to be able to differentiate), but I've learned that instead of comparing where I am to where others are, it's better to compare where I am to where I want to be.

There is a big difference between being *the* best and being *my* best. Every choice we make leads us closer to (or pulls us

---

13 John Adams, deputy director/COO of the Biosphere 2 project at Arizona State University, email to author, December 24, 2024.

I've learned that instead of comparing where I am to where others are, it's better to compare where I am to where I want to be.

away from) the person we desire to be. Those choices that bring us closer are worth the energy it takes to remain standing.

Growth Reflection

In the Past: Has a mental shift helped you reevaluate or perhaps calibrate what is important to you? Can you tie it back to an experience or a set of experiences?

In the Present: Are you facing resistance in an area of your life? How can the resistance make you a stronger, more capable person?

Thoughts

FINAL WORD

IT IS FAIR TO SAY you know quite a bit about me, but that wasn't my main objective. More important, I hope you learned something about yourself. Perhaps you had an aha moment that offered some clarity on how you approach challenges or interact with others. Maybe you remembered some of your experiences and the nuggets of wisdom gained from them. You may have even had a moment of inspiration as you recalled how you overcame an obstacle.

No experience is wasted if we are willing to learn. No hurt can paralyze you or make you bitter unless you allow it. I know that it is not easy to get up after we've been knocked down, but we get stronger every time we do. Problems don't get easier. We get better and outgrow them. The best version of you is on the other side of not giving up, not making excuses, and not blaming others. I will even argue that you cannot achieve the best version of yourself without hardship or challenges. The path of least resistance is paved with mediocrity. Your path is yours, and while you do not have to walk it alone, I encourage you to own it!

I have learned more from challenges than successes, but taking a few minutes to evaluate what led to a desirable outcome can help replicate the success. Asking a question as simple as what went well can help identify key contributors, and adding "why," as in why it went well, will flush out factors that were both in and out of your control.

I will leave you with a nugget that may help on this adventure we call life. By now, you realize there are several things that we cannot control. Life has many variables in its ecosystem. It is unrealistic to believe that we can control every outcome (or input), but we can choose to own our part in them.

Let's focus on what you can control with Ownership Outcomes.

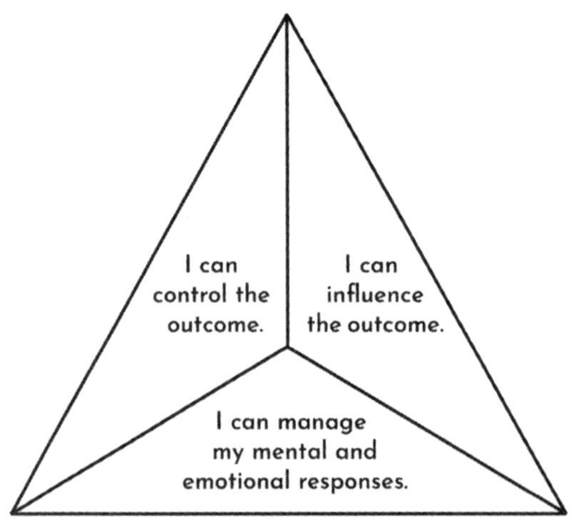

FINAL WORD

Learning What You Can Manage

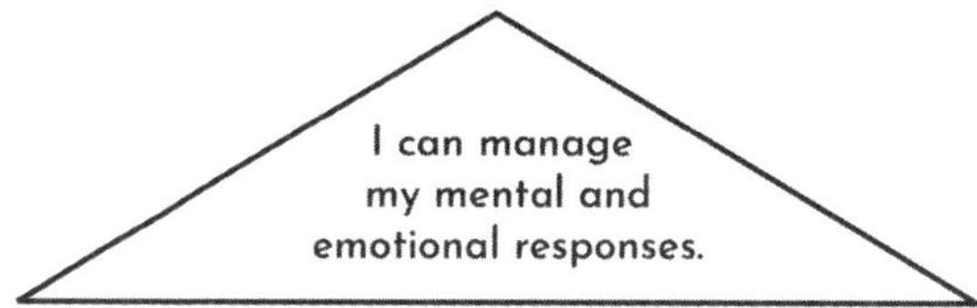

Learning to manage our mental and emotional responses is foundational for learning what we can control and what we can influence. The ability to manage how we process and perceive our environment (our thoughts about external factors), the emotions that impact interactions with others, and the thoughts about ourselves directly impacts our quality of life.

At any given time, we are in one of three states: ignorance, awareness, or denial. Obviously, ignorance lacks awareness and denial lacks acknowledgment. Awareness is the most powerful and pivotal state because this is where a decision must be made. We can never go back to ignorance once we are aware, but we can choose denial.

In a state of awareness, we get to determine our actions. (Inaction can be an action when used to de-escalate or make a statement.) Oftentimes, awareness starts the cascade of emotions that color our perceptions—positive or negative.

The power lies in getting to choose how we manage our thoughts, our responses, and how we engage with others. The management of this outcome impacts all other outcomes.

It is important to recognize the difference between a hard moment, a challenging day, a tough season in life, and the triggers or patterns that initiate them. We have the ability to choose our perspective for that moment, day, or season. Reassembling the letter my dad wrote and then reading it was a hard moment for me. Seeing him in person for the first time after I read it was a challenging day. Three years of not talking to him afterward was a tough season. We don't have to allow a moment to turn into a season.

Let's make this practical for today because for some of us, managing our mental and emotional responses for a more productive outcome feels as if we are fighting against our very nature. First, we must be aware of the emotion driving the response. Then, we need to identify what caused it.

- Is there something or someone who irritates, annoys, or offends you?
- Does your mood change in an unpleasant way when you encounter this something or someone?
- Is your behavior impacted?
- Do you feel physiological changes?
- Is it fair to say that you are having an emotional response?

Obviously, emotions such as happiness, excitement, amusement, and even relief can drive a response as well. Typically, there is little concern for undesirable outcomes with these emotions, but sometimes even they can put us in precarious situations if we don't manage them properly.

If our mental and emotional responses have the potential to produce the outcome we do not want, we can ask ourselves, *How can I approach this situation differently to achieve the outcome I do want? How can I achieve a better result or interaction?*

Yes . . . I am assuming that you want the best outcome, because if you are reading this book, you want to become the best version of yourself or you want to help someone become the best version of themself.

Think of challenging situations you have encountered, what you learned from them, and perhaps what you would do differently.

- What can you borrow from lessons you have already learned to manage your mental and emotional responses for the outcome you prefer?
- What can you learn from the experiences of others?
- Are you able to honor what you feel and temper your emotion for more sound decision-making?

As a general personal rule, I have learned not to make permanent decisions in temporary situations. You may find this helpful as well. Momentary stressors and short-lived circumstances can cause us to forget their fleeting nature. Challenging *now* does not mean challenging *always*, and we must be careful about allowing an emotional impact to dictate long-term decisions and outcomes.

Learning What You Can Control

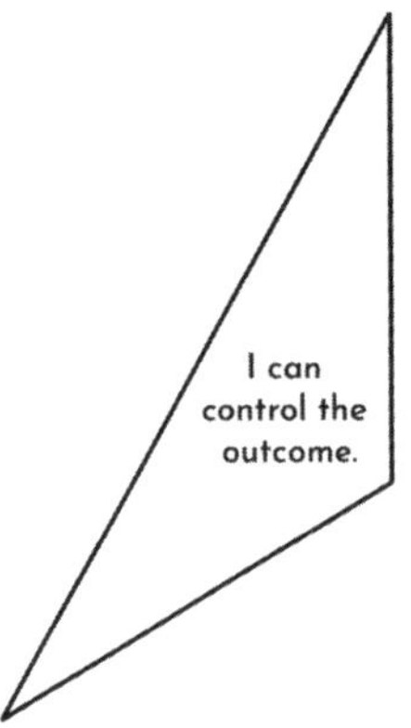

There are very few things outside of personal decisions that we can control. The outcomes of the decisions that are within our direct control are predictable because the decisions rest solely with us.

The average adult makes thousands of decisions per day. Many of those decisions are made on autopilot, but we do have direct control over them. Something as simple as hitting the snooze button in the morning is a decision, and that decision may determine if you are prompt or running behind (and maybe a little frazzled as you start your day). Outside of extenuating circumstances, arriving on time is within our control. Other examples include what we say, our behaviors, what we choose to consume (taste, sight, auditory), who we choose to spend time with, where we decide to work, and so on. The immediate results of these decisions are "control outcomes." They are the direct outcome of individual will—what we choose to do or not do.

I may decide not to tie my shoes today. I control that decision. The outcome is I walk around with untied shoes. This leads us to something we are all familiar with—consequences. If I don't tie my shoes, we shouldn't be surprised if I trip and fall.

Remember my summer of water gun fun? I could have said no. I would not have been a part of the battle that day, but I also would have avoided the hole in my foot, the trip to the emergency room, and so on and so on.

A control outcome—the result of what we choose to do—often impacts an "influence outcome"—these are less predictable. Arriving on time, being a team player, and having a constructive attitude have the potential to positively impact (or influence) another person's decisions about us in the same way arriving late, being hard to work with, and having a toxic disposition can in the opposite way. The good news is, although we cannot control every outcome, we can control our effort and the consistency in how we show up.

What does this look like today? Let's keep it simple. Think about your next conversation. You get to choose your words, the tone and volume of the delivery, and other nuances that affect how the message is received. The choices made here will influence how the recipient responds. Managing the foundational outcome—your mental and emotional responses—can make the interaction more palatable when the conversation is hard.

It is also important to acknowledge that control outcomes impact others in many areas. No person exists in isolation. Our health is a great example of this. We can control food and beverage choices, physical activity, time outdoors, etc. These decisions are within our direct control and impact the quality of our health. Our health may enhance or impair the quality of our relationships. The health of many individuals affects the collective health of a community.

Another example of a control outcome is where we choose to spend our time. Consider the return on investment from reading a book every month that fosters learning and generating new ideas. Some people read a book a week. The investment in your own development pays dividends in multiples. The knowledge gained is immediate. The outcome of an improved life and better opportunities is a well-earned byproduct of the investment in yourself.

Learning What You Can Influence

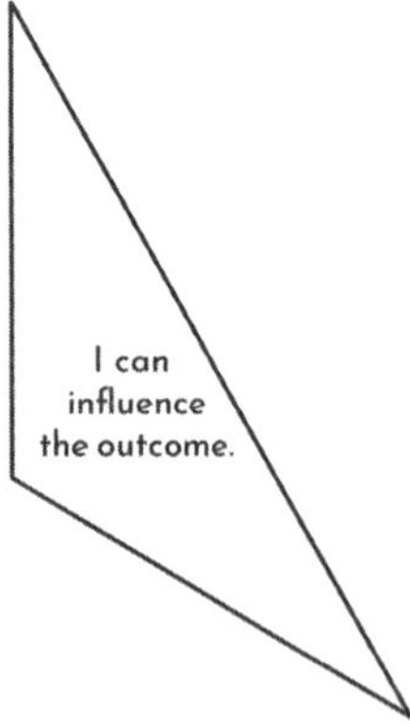

These outcomes are not predictable or guaranteed, and they are not solely owned by us. We have the potential to affect other parties in the decision-making process, but unlike the control outcome, a direct result of our individual choice, we do not have final say or authority over the end result.

If anyone other than you has a part in the outcome—if another person's will has an impact on the equation—you do not have full control of the final product or decision. Your influence may be so great that it seems as if you have control, but do not deceive yourself into thinking that your control is absolute. Many people have learned this when the result did not turn out as anticipated—whether from miscommunication, a change of heart, or even deception.

Learning where we have influence (versus control) can be a game changer in how we set expectations and engage with others. Relieve yourself of the stress of believing you can control other people. You can certainly influence them (for good) and help them on their journey. Your influence may even change someone's life in the most profound ways, but they get to make the choices that ultimately lead to the change.

In the professional arena, we can collaborate for meaningful business outcomes, passionately persuading others to achieve results that impact communities and generations. Influence is powerful, so let's make it applicable.

- Is there someone you want to help succeed?
- Is there something you are passionate about that you want to see improve?

- Who are the people you need to connect with to start the process?

You cannot control the situation or person, but you can influence them. Remember my mental reset for the meaning of the word "ambition": When a woman I respected reestablished the meaning in a way that finally connected for me, I was persuaded to embrace her improved definition. Imagine if I had not had the encounters that challenged my mindset and encouraged me to define the word correctly. I might have been tempted to play small for a lack of embracing truth.

May we all be blessed with someone in our life who positively influences us and challenges us to stretch beyond our self-inflicted limits!

Empowered

Now you get to decide what you will do with the awareness and insights you have gained through the stories and exercises in these pages. Emotions such as anger, fear, and happiness can be modulated once we acknowledge them, and now you have a better understanding of whether you can control or influence an outcome. Decisions such as how we treat others, where and how we decide to utilize our talents, and personal investments in our growth are owned by us, but the effect on others extends beyond us. We will make many decisions in our lifetime, and I would argue most of them will be made without much thought, but several can be made with intentionality.

Understanding what we influence versus what we control grants us a degree of liberation. It also gifts us with wisdom in how we can choose to engage in order to impact the outcome. The best part is this: We are empowered to lead ourselves well.

It is worth restating that no experience is wasted if we are willing to learn from it. Learning is a lifelong process. We never arrive; we are always on the journey. Every day is an opportunity. Embrace the challenges; they are a great teacher and the fuel for your greatest impact. Every ounce of joy, pain, frustration, wonder, sadness, love, disgust, and even shame brought you to this day. You don't get to live it again; it is a gift.

Resilience must be earned; you cannot get it from reading about it, talking about it, or seeing it. You must live it—like the trees growing stronger in the wind.

You could have been born anywhere, at any time, in any place, but here you are. How wonderful is that? Have the courage to be yourself as you evolve to become the best version of you.

Do not live in the past; allow the past to inform your future, as we did in these pages. Be aware of the dual nature of each moment. Live fully present and understand that today's decisions impact your tomorrows.

Do not accept limitations. Walk with awareness. And gratitude.

Your story is still being written. Make it a good one.

—TORI

Ownership Outcomes

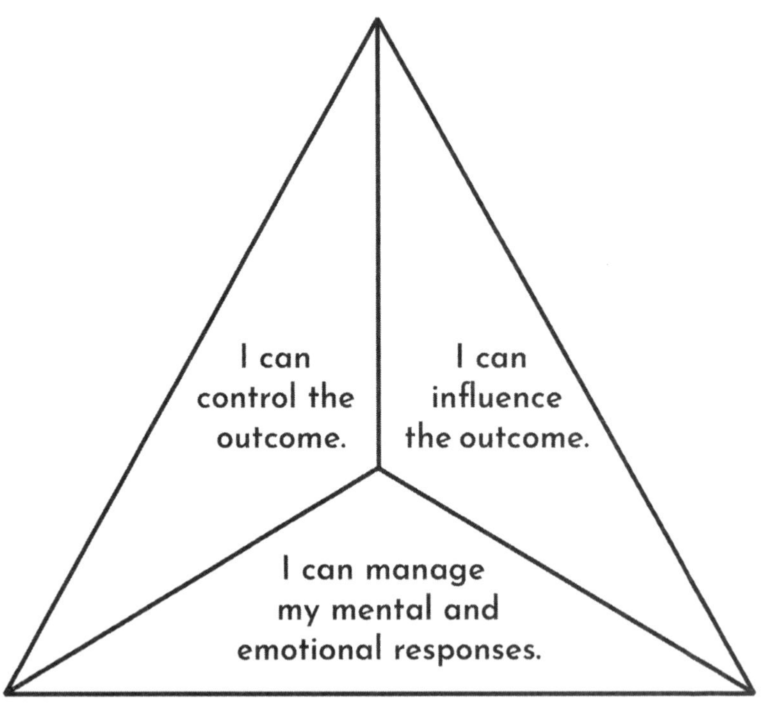

ABOUT THE AUTHOR

TORI DACOSTA is a businesswoman, coach, author, and speaker who focuses on empowering leaders to lead themselves well. Her work centers on helping individuals create impactful lives through the transformative power of ownership. As a leader in a Fortune 50 company and a mentor, Tori brings insight into the value of learning through experiences as she inspires others to become the best version of themselves.

Tori holds multiple degrees and professional designations, including an executive MBA from Emory University, a bachelor's degree from Appalachian State University, and an associate's degree from the University of South Carolina at Sumter.

She lives in North Carolina with her husband, Mike, and enjoys spending time with their two children. She also enjoys running, almost anything outdoors, and laughter.